THE POWER OF ME

THE POWER OF ME

Spiritual Tools for the Great Awakening

DIANNE HODGES

The Power of Me, Spiritual Tools for the Great Awakening

For information, contact: Omniverse Publishing, LLC, P. O. Box 4871, Sedona, Arizona 86340-4871 • www.omniversepublishingsedona.com

Library of Congress Control Number: 2015944901
Publisher: Omniverse Publishing, LLC

ISBN: 978-0-692-45236-3

First Printing, June 2015

Graphics and cover design by Thunder Mountain Design
Author Portrait and cross symbol by Ed Hodges
Editing by Catherine Rourke and Katharine Ferguson

I lovingly dedicate this book to
my husband, Ed, and my daughter, Erin,
who chose to walk by my side witnessing
and supporting my journey to
self-empowerment and mastery.

I love and cherish you both.

ABOUT THE COVER

The central image on the book cover is open to many interpretations. A few saw the spiral and envisioned a womb of the God-Source or the fabric of eternity; some focused on the butterfly and imagined transformation and metamorphosis. On the left side of the spiral is the silhouette of a woman's face appearing and disappearing as in an optical illusion. The feather depicts a spiritual connection invoking power, strength, and gentleness. The feather remains a significant symbol for me personally, as I asked spirit for a pictorial representation for my book cover *The Power of Me.*

The image of a feather burst into my head one day while doing household chores. It sometimes happens that way, when you least expect it… just like the topics and chapter titles for this book, which flowed from my mind one morning out of the blue, in the parking lot of a grocery store. Whenever I ponder a question or a problem, I eventually receive an answer intuitively recognizing the truth of it by the way it makes me feel. I joyously marvel at these synchronistic moments when spirit responds with answers to my questions or assists me with my life's journey.

According to Native American legends, the feather represents an antenna to the spiritual world. It is believed that the feather helps you connect to your spiritual self, where you receive spiritual guidance, strength, and clarity. The feather is a symbol for higher wisdom, truth, gentleness and light. The eagle is the most honored symbol in the bird kingdom that the American Indians revere so much.

"The eagle carries your prayers directly to the creator." That's how a Native

American man explained it to me once. We also see this icon in the wings of an angel. That day I also saw the image of a childhood cartoon about a baby elephant named "Dumbo," a Walt Disney character.

A feather helped him overcome his fear and discover his uniqueness. His big ears turned out to be the source of his special gift of flight. Dumbo flew past his fears and rose up to heights beyond his wildest dreams. The feather represented his connection between his physical and spiritual self. For a brief moment, he believed the feather made him fly. However, he quickly learned that the strength and ability to fly were within him all along. He just didn't realize he had these hidden talents.

A *spiritual feather* is the connection between your physical world and your higher consciousness. Let's pretend I am giving you a spiritual feather in the form of this book to hold close to your heart. It is a tool to guide you, to give you the confidence to fly past your fears, to believe in yourself, and to know who you truly are.

CONTENTS

FOREWORD

The Power of Me graciously illustrates Dianne Hodges's inner passion to not only make the world a better place, but also compassionately guide those who have similar intentions but are not sure where to begin. She employs her wisdom and healing methods throughout this book, which is a clear, concise, and straightforward "how-to" approach for accepting and loving oneself.

Dianne utilizes her own experiences and life lessons, as well as those of other teachers. She does so without judgment, without ego, and with a refreshing sense of humor. *The Power of Me* is well versed and an easy-to-read manual for those beginning on their journey as well as those who have been traversing this path for many years. We found her motto, "to live one's truth at all costs," to be a powerful reminder of a daily practice that requires conscious discipline.

Chapter 13, in particular, caught our attention. It reminds us of the importance of trusting who we are in spite of contradicting external messages. Dianne clearly writes how vital it is to "reclaim" the self, and she provides the reader with step-by-step methods of assistance, thus clarifying and defining her title, *The Power of Me.*

Chapter 10 addresses the handling of fear, including fear of death. Dianne references this very human emotion in a non-judgmental way. From her examples, the reader can understand how to move through fear rather than become mired in it. No matter what age or life experience, we can find ourselves in unexpected situations triggering sudden fear and it can often feel paralyzing.

Dianne's insight and practical "how-to" approach can assist us in moving through our fears while not "getting stuck" in them. To acknowledge that emotion gracefully without attaching to it is mastery. This chapter provides the groundwork for accomplishing such mastery.

During many a night and day, the three of us have hashed over our life lessons, spoken vulnerably about our challenges, and pondered a more conscious way of forgiving mistakes and learning the human lessons. Dianne devotes Chapter 21, "The Test," as a gentle nudge for us to remember who we truly are and refuse to become "victimized" by life's challenges. Her definitions of achievement in mastering our personal tests are measured by "how well you have acted, how much you have reacted, how you thought, how you loved, and how much you gave to others." Read that chapter for more details.

We met Dianne almost thirteen years ago and have supported one another and learned from one another ever since. When we first met Dianne, it felt like a reunion of sorts—the remembrance of a special soul from eons ago. It was as if before our energies took "form," we had whispered to one another, "See you in Sedona in the 21st century, and let's remind each other what is real and what is illusion."

Both of us continue to be impressed by Dianne's self-deprecating and funny sense of humor, her enormous capacity to be of service, and her wonderment at why so many individuals choose suffering over healing.

As a massage therapist, Dianne has healed us many times through her therapeutic gifts as well as her enlightened spiritual insight. She has the unique ability to release her ego, and become a vessel of healing, a channel of empathy, and a wise seer. Her quest has always been to "reclaim" herself in order that she may assist others in "claiming" themselves. She has adeptly demonstrated this throughout her career.

Often the three of us have sat over coffee to reflect and probe the depths of many a human issue. Clarity always ensues, whether a deeper understanding of this world of duality or how to make practical a spiritual philosophy that benefits the "greater good."

We know that all readers spanning many different age groups will highly benefit from Dianne's in-depth writing and rich life experience. Her gifts as a writer, a healer, and a humorist are all prevalent in this important book. It is with honor and love that we highly recommend *The Power of Me!*

- *James Recore, M.A., Counseling; Spiritual Teacher and Healer*
- *Brenda Recore, M.A., Psychology/Education; Life Coach and Group Facilitator*

PREFACE

Thinking: the talking of the soul with itself.

– Plato

I wish I had a book like this when I was younger; my life would have been so much easier!

I have always had an untamed imagination and an inquisitive, searching mind with a thousand questions and no one to answer them. I wanted to know the meaning of life and why I am here on earth.

"What is my purpose? What's next?" These were the questions I often asked. This turmoil caused so much stress and confusion in my life. It was enough to drive anyone crazy.

I always had a sense of what the answers were, but was never really sure. I never got confirmation of the truth. I could have used a practical manual to help me with this awakening process. I needed something to guide me down my spiritual path, through all of life's twists and turns.

Was there another alternative that could summarize for me how to manage my life with power, ease, and grace, without compromising my integrity?

Something that could serve as a guidebook during all those challenging times: a disagreement with a friend or spouse, an ethical issue at work, bouts of unemployment or illness, loss of a loved one or a home, or even simple everyday events like losing the car keys.

I wish there had been a go-to handbook for all of life's trials and tribulations, to show me how to come out on top without feeling trampled or stepping on others' toes.

I was lost.

I groped, I stumbled, and I fell.

If I had a book like this to help years ago, I could have saved myself so much stress and confusion. I might have had a different perspective on those situations and understood the bigger picture behind them.

Instead of buying into the drama and kicking and screaming at times in my life, maybe I could have chosen a different way to believe, behave, and react; if only I had known to look within myself for answers rather than outside of me.

But I learned. Now, here in this book I am going to share with you everything I wish I had known thirty or forty years ago that could have made my life so much simpler and prevented so much anguish.

Since I had to figure it all out for myself, it dawned on me that I should sum up everything I've learned the hard way so maybe it could benefit others, someone like you. If I can do that for you, then all my pain will have been more rewarding and worthwhile.

Since there are few road maps for young adults and spiritual initiates to show them how to find their own path and identify their own truths, I decided a spiritual manual would be helpful for learning how to create a life of peace and harmony.

The purpose of ***The Power of Me*** is to teach and inspire you, the "student of the divine,"[1] to search for your own personal spiritual path, and inner truth. It is a "journey to your own heart," as my spiritual guide and teacher Dr. James Martin Peebles* always says. It offers a pathway to discover your true self, and to understand your deeper purpose and the endless, inner drive to answer all your questions.

"Who am I and why am I here?"

"What do I do now?"

"Where do I go from here?"

"Who is God?"

I won't give you the answers to those deep questions we all have, but I will assist you in your search for the solutions. I can't promise that it will be easy. You have to do the work.

This journey will let you open the doorway to your spiritual heart, let you peek in and discover your true self, and provide you with the answers to a happy and fulfilling life.

This book is an introduction and, perhaps, a new beginning that allows you to move beyond the drama and distractions of everyday life and to understand the relationship between what is really going on in your inner and outer worlds. It is one of many that you will read over time to expand your knowledge and understanding of yourself.

I encourage you to keep searching beyond this book, since we really never stop learning. It is a continuous search but, at some point, you will find a place within yourself where you will finally feel comfortable in your skin. You will know when you have found that place of peace and joy. You will know what works and what does not work in your life.

Within these pages, I encourage you, the awakening student, to walk down the path of self-discovery using your vast imagination to seek the divine within, no matter what your religion or belief system. I encourage you to live a life of love, joy, peace, and harmony, by truly knowing and understanding a more expansive view of your life, and the future of this school here on earth at this great moment of the great awakening in our galactic* history.

This is an exciting time to be a human on earth. You are part of a Great Awakening* that is occurring now throughout the entire universe where all awakened beings shift consciousness and expand at once to a higher vibratory rate by moving from the Third Dimension* to the Fifth Dimension.* Sometimes this major shift in consciousness is referred to as Ascension.*

Together we will explore some metaphysical concepts and "what if" questions in these chapters to facilitate a better understanding of the "God-self," * or the Divine within us. This book also offers you a gigantic pep talk on how to *be* in the world. It introduces several tools to facilitate your own process in your personal awakening so you can be part of the "Great Universal Awakening."*

Many of the concepts I discuss already exist in hundreds of books. However, this one is unique in that it is geared for the searching mind, with everything explained in simple language that is easily understood, yet challenging to the status quo. It also highlights examples from my own life story to help you better understand some of these concepts, with some tears and laughter, too.

When you study and absorb the concepts in this book, your everyday challenges such as your job, school, or relationships with your friends, family, spouse, or partner may reflect less drama, struggle, and pain.

As I look back at my life, I could have had an easier time with my family members if I had understood them from a more compassionate frame of mind. I would have shown more love and forgiveness, instead of holding back. Perhaps I could have gone to my job with confidence and joy in my heart rather than feeling stress and frustration.

Take a moment to look at your life. I know you are probably having similar experiences. If you could look at your father, for example, and find a way to just love and forgive him and realize that he taught you many lessons such as patience, empathy, and forgiveness, then you have made a huge shift in your personal awakening.

Can you imagine how this small action—your personal shift of consciousness—clears out the old thought patterns and brings in the thought patterns of love and appreciation? This, my fellow students, reverberates throughout the whole universe. This is how we go within to deal with our world's many challenges.

Consider how profound and powerful this small single act can be, knowing you just created positive movement in the universe!

As I developed my spiritual maturity over the years, what I have discovered is that the path to knowing the answers lies within me. I just needed to acknowledge it and trust it. That is my true power. This is "the **Power of Me**."

When you arrive at the place of spiritual self-awareness, knowing your truth and divinity deep within your soul, you are "awake." You become an awakened soul.

How do you get there?

Each of our paths is different. There is no one-size-fits-all solution. Your spiritual quest is to awaken to your personal truth along with the Grand Awakening of all people collectively uniting, transforming our planet into Heaven on Earth along with other realms of the universe. Be a part of this quest and fulfill your life's dreams as you absorb the various concepts presented here.

I was encouraged and inspired to write this book by the many teachings of Dr. Peebles, who is channeled by Summer Bacon.* It never occurred to me to write a book about my personal philosophies and my lifetime of lessons until Dr. Peebles suggested it.

I pondered this notion for a while, realizing that I certainly did have many amazing opportunities and experiences in my outer and inner spiritual worlds. Why not share them, if it would assist people on their own personal journey? As a minister with a journalism degree, I could write a life-changing book.

Even before Dr. Peebles suggested I write this, I always felt there was a message that needed to be revealed to people, and mainly to the younger generation, who hunger for a spiritual connection. For a long time, I have also experienced an inner urging that adults need to prepare their children for what lies ahead. That is why I include a special chapter for parents at the end of the book.

As we clear ourselves and refine these concepts, we light the way for our children. They learn from our example and demonstration on how to be in the world and how to express love, compassion and forgiveness without holding back. As our children learn these concepts (and many already know), our collective future will be one of peace as we ascend from the Third to the Fifth Dimension.

I intuitively know that the children being born now are more advanced than their predecessors. They have different needs, desires, and goals. Many of these children already know the answers. We need to support, encourage, and nurture them without hindering them.

Adapting these concepts and adding your own intuitive principles can change your life and the lives of your children. You will find new ways to move out of the negativity surrounding you. You will feel your heart open and bring in more love. It is subtle and takes some time, but you will notice it one day as you work to clear away the old patterns and bring in the new ones. You will feel calmer and more confident as you cope with all of life's challenges with greater ease.

With this in mind… one day as I was sitting in a grocery store parking lot, a flow of words suddenly emerged out of the blue. I scribbled the topics and names of all the chapters for this book right there in that parking lot.

I originally started writing this book for young teenagers. However, I soon realized that each of us could awaken at any time, so I expanded my reading audience to embrace all ages and levels of spiritual awareness and maturity. Therefore, some of these concepts are very simple in explanation, and I use my personal explorations and experiences to demonstrate how this awakening process within unfolds.

A couple of writing years later, struggling with the main theme and title of the book, I was again encouraged by Dr. Peebles. As we began our channeling session one day, I explained to him that I was very busy discovering "the power of me."

He responded: "That sounds like a good title for a book."

It was the "aha" moment for the title and theme for the work that appears before you now.

As I mentioned above, I know from my own experience that this type of information would have been very helpful for me at a very impressionable and vulnerable time in my life. I had to feel my way along, many times, all alone, by learning the hard way.

To assist the searching mind, this unique book explains many spiritual and metaphysical concepts in simple language that challenges many of the standard norms. Perhaps it will be a beginning for you or confirm what you may already intuitively know. Sometimes we just need a little confirmation on what is happening or what we perceive.

The releasing of the "old" and opening up to the "new" is a birthing process and often very challenging at any age for both young and old. But there is *light* at the end of the proverbial tunnel, as they say. After a long and sometimes painful process discovering who you truly are, a magnificent birth occurs—a new life, beginning with the first breath and first beat of the heart when you discover that God is within you.

At the end of the book, I share my perceptions of the collective notion that all of us, including our Planet Earth, are headed for a grand Ascension. It will be magnificent. You are part of it. You need to ask to be a part of it. You need to be prepared. This book will provide you with some tips and tools to ease you into this process, with an open and loving mind, so we all achieve our goal to return home together as *One*.

Once you start the awakening process and begin your journey to your personal and planetary ascension, I encourage you to search out other information, other books, movies, teachers, and mentors— whatever you need—to join us in the Great Awakening. Ask for the wisdom to come to you and it will unfold right before your eyes.

I wish to help you expand your thinking and gain a firm foundation and understanding of your gifts and true God-self, ideally at a much earlier age. The time is now for the Great Awakening and you will want to be a part of it. It is your choice.

So here it is: everything I wish I knew when I was starting out on the spiritual path. Tap into your inherent desire to seek the truth and choose to be a part of the great awakening by adapting this book's concepts and tools into your life.

Enjoy the journey to your *Oneness* with the divine!

– Dianne Hodges, Sedona, Arizona

[Wherever a raised number[1] appears, please refer to the Footnotes at the end of the book. An asterisk* means that word or term can be found in the Glossary for further explanation.]

ACKNOWLEDGMENTS

The many profound kernels of information for this book came from numerous sources and teachers who have entered into my life experiences. I thank all of you for your contribution in guiding me through this web of life, whether we met personally or through your book(s). These kernels have all weaved their way into my mind to become my truth.

In the following pages, I have shared my truth with you, as I understand it today. I am still exploring and evolving, because I do not have all the answers YET. I am still learning and will continue to learn forever. Our education never stops—only our school or, rather, our plane of existence changes. The names, the faces, and the personalities change but the souls and their messages of truth remain the constant. We only need to be curious enough to search for them and then experience them.

I wish to thank my very first spiritual teacher, Orpheus Phylos, a well-known author, teacher, artist, and channel for Archangel Michael. My first psychic "reading"* with Michael changed my life and opened doors into my inner world instantly.

I then met Angela DeBry, Ph.D., a gifted teacher, spiritual channel, Dean of Education and Vice President of the Board of Directors of the Sacred Foundations, Inc, which holds that no single set of fixed rules is applicable to all individuals in their spiritual quest. She taught all of us who were ready to learn many wondrous things about our world, our cosmos, and ourselves. She has channeled many entities from the galactic federation* and beyond.

With that initial information from both Orpheus and Angela, I really came out of the "box" of religion and worldliness, which expanded my thinking in ways I never thought possible.

However, I feel that my first book has hardly touched upon the expansive wisdom that exists in the many dimensions, but it is our reality—or, rather, my reality nonetheless—here in the Third Dimension on Planet Earth at this time.

I wish to thank my dear friend Katharine Ferguson, who introduced me to Orpheus and Angela. It was her first introduction to the world of metaphysics that cracked open my psyche and fast-forwarded my life's journey into a new direction. I especially wish to thank her for her spiritual guidance and final editing and polishing of this book.

I also wish to acknowledge and thank Summer Bacon, who channels Dr. James Martin Peebles. She is a role model for me as she shared her authenticity and integrity with all us who attended her lectures. Dr. Peebles' constant and enduring messages of love, compassion and appreciation helped me to go even deeper into myself.

Alijandra, wherever you are these days, I wish to thank you for teaching me how to feel the energies and heal myself. Your talent and wisdom is profound, and I appreciate you.

I also wish to thank my family who has been there for me when I needed you at the most appropriate and timely moments and who felt firsthand, (and put up with) my rebellious and independent nature. I especially want to thank my husband, Ed, and my daughter, Erin, who have watched me grow, change, and wondered many times if Mom was going crazy. Your love and support through the ups and downs of this experience of finding my truth is so appreciated. You have no idea how important it was for me to know you were there loving me and supporting me no matter what weird thing I came up with. I love you both.

I wish to thank my parents who tried very hard to teach me to fit in to the ways of the earth. I know it was a challenge as I fought you every inch of the way. You still managed to teach me to stand up for myself, to be strong, and to talk my way out of anything. I love you.

To my brother, Brad, and my sister, Janet—well, what can I say other than it has been one heck of a journey together. All I ever wanted was to do it my way. You both put up with my antics and I thank you for that and I love you too.

The following people have also touched me with their wisdom, love, friendship, and encouragement at just the right time when I needed them. I thank you and I love you: Melanie Marani, Greg and Gayle Siegler, Shirley Jenne, Michelle Jenne, Barbara Van DerVeer, Steve Waites, Connie Cotton, Dawn Adams, Lynne Barbas, Joyce Williams, Maia Kincaid, Guy Worth, Dan and Virginia Barrow, Yvonne Haskins, Phyllis Johnson, Kathy Stahmann, Rhonda Bierman. Thank you, George Tsukuda, my old friend. We helped each other when we needed it, if only for a brief time.

To my editor, Catherine Rourke, thank you. The birthing process of this book would never have happened without your loving and supportive guidance. The mammoth leap we made from the start to the finished work astounds me. You taught me so much and showed me the way to believe in myself as a writer.

And finally, special thanks to Brenda and James Recore who have enough love, wisdom, understanding, and patience to fill the universe. I cherish your friendship. Your love and guidance was invaluable to me.

I thank you and love you all.

I also wish to thank the many authors who wrote books of wisdom that touched my heart and shaped my thinking over the years. Often I would be pondering some profound question about the universe and, within a short time, I would open your book and you would give me the answer I was seeking. Thank you for sharing your truth and wisdom. It is appreciated.

Thank you, again, to all who touched my life.

INTRODUCTION

Never forget that you are one of a kind. Never forget that if there weren't any need for you in all your uniqueness to be on this earth, you wouldn't be here in the first place. And never forget, no matter how overwhelming life's challenges and problems seem to be, that one person can make a difference in the world. In fact, it is always because of one person that all the changes that matter in the world come about. So be that one person.

- Buckminster Fuller

The wild ride to your spiritual heart is an exciting and never-ending adventure. Once you shine a light on your soul and ask "What is my journey on earth really about?" your life will never be the same. It can be like a roller coaster ride with many ups and downs but—wow!—what a fantastic ride it is. This spiritual adventure is life altering and holds all the answers to your problems if you are willing to do the search and do the work.

This book can save you many years of anguish and struggle as I share with you my many lessons and revelations. Some will be new to you, and others are obvious, yet perhaps I add a new twist or perspective to your current thought patterns. If I can save you several years of strife in one easy read, sharing with you the many ground rules with a step-by-step approach, then I have accomplished what I set out to do.

The structure of this book is divided into two parts. In Part 1, I explain the many tools, concepts, and personal experiences for the spiritual seeker. In Part 2, I will portray what the Great Awakening means for you and how you can join the rest of humanity in this monumental shift that is about to take place.

I will describe how this is all going to unfold in this book. In some places we delve into theory, but I'll try not to be overly academic. Many concepts are introduced, which may be difficult to grasp at first, especially if new to this area of study. I will use some examples from my own life so you can see how it works and offer you some tools for how you can apply them to your own everyday life. Some concepts are reiterated throughout the book to emphasize their significance, but also to put them into different contexts and examples to facilitate your comprehension.

I've also included a special Glossary to define many terms and concepts for you, as well as a summary of principles to help you understand everything—simply and easily—the way I wish I could have accessed this wisdom decades ago. So, wherever you see an asterisk or raised number, you will find further information in the Glossary and Footnotes at the end of the book to answer all your questions.

In Part 1, we will explore the basic tools, philosophies, and laws of the universe. This will give you the basic foundation you need to begin to embrace "the Power of Me." Examples from my own journey will offer a demonstration on how to apply them to your own path. I will begin by exploring the many possibilities of the Divine, using such terms as "gods in training" and "co-creator," as well as the "universal laws of Love, Light, Free Will, Balance, and Reincarnation."*

In my book I refer to "god*" in lower case meaning "divinity" and not "idolatry." "God*" is capitalized when referring to the Creator, and I prefer to use "it" instead of "him" for that reference. For greater clarity, I refer to the "Big God" simply as "God," and also use the pronoun "it." The lowercased "god" represents you and me. These terms and other uses are also explained for you in the Glossary at the end of the book.

Next we examine the many ways in which we can be empowered through love, self-responsibility, forgiveness, overcoming our fears, understanding our dreams, and mastering our ego and intuition. I offer suggestions on how to meditate and learn to listen to your spirit-guided voice within. There is also a chapter on the paranormal since many people encounter this challenge and are not sure what to do about it.

The final chapters outline how to be, how not to be, and, of course, the important role that relationships play as we twist and turn together on our mutual journeys.

In Part 2, the Great Awakening is portrayed, as I understand it now. Please keep in mind that this is an ever-evolving story as we collectively go through this birthing process. The potential and probability lines for this awakening are continually changing as we learn, grow, manifest, and surrender to this grand plan. Perhaps, this information will expand your belief system and allow you to open your mind to think outside the box.

My interpretation represents one of many. That is okay since we all search for the truth. As I do the research and learn more, I am sure my interpretation will change and expand. It is a continuous flow since we are each given just the right amount of information and assistance when we are ready at the most appropriate and perfect moment. I encourage you to seek out other points of view on this exciting change that is unfolding here on our Planet Earth and the entire universe.

If, at any time, my words end up being your words and I have not quoted you properly, please contact the publisher so you receive proper credit for your wisdom. When I combine my lifetime of learning into a book, it is hard for me to remember all the sources of information. I apologize in advance if that has happened; it is unintentional. We are all here to share our knowledge as we each interpret it. Our knowledge represents our love and service to ourselves and to mankind.

In some of these writings, I know I am getting a bit political, such as in mentioning war issues or oil spills. It is hard to separate politics from life. It was Mary Travers of the "Peter, Paul and Mary" folksingers who once said, in reference to the group's political statements in its songs—"It is not about politics; it is about ethics."

I do apologize if I offend anyone, but we all have opinions, beliefs, philosophies, and ethics. I am just sharing a part of me with you. Before I can do that, I really need to know myself on a deep level. (As I write, I reveal who I am one layer at a time). Who am I really? I need to ask that question of myself seriously. When I figure it out, that is when I truly will know the line between me, my emotions and someone else.

It is my lesson in life—part of my contract—to figure out who I am and learn about the Power of Me. Am I really this sensitive loving, peaceful person speaking her truth or that angry, sad, frustrated person? I believe I am a sensitive, loving person. Those other emotions are not mine. They belong to other people and perhaps even Mother Earth.

We all become angry from time to time. I will own those feelings that are actually my own and work them out in my own way and time. It is amazing synchronicity when we have an issue surface in our life and we pick up a book and read about a solution, or someone comes along and says just the right thing that gives us the answer we are seeking.

Remember to listen for those messages. That is your soul, guides, and teachers guiding you to find the answers. (It may be part of the contracts you have with each other, in which one agrees to come into your life at just the right time to help you with a problem or a question.)

In these chapters, I will differentiate between your personal graduation and the collective universal Ascension or what is generally called the Great Awakening. There is a test we must all acknowledge and pass in order to move beyond duality to a place of knowingness and awareness of our universal mind in order to expand our consciousness. And there is no failing grade, only more learning and clearing opportunities.

Why are we doing this? We are old souls returning to clear the old ways through various cycles to bring in the new ways of being—new levels of consciousness—so we can all live happy, fulfilling lives along with our precious Mother Earth, and possibly with a little help from our celestial friends. They are all calling upon you now to do your part. Your soul is calling upon you to wake up and be part of this Grand Awakening now. This is a fantastic time to be alive on earth during these amazing times where all your aspirations and dreams will come true!

PART ONE

Basic Tools, Philosophies, and Laws of the Universe

CHAPTER 1

Our Journey Begins

Do not follow where the path may lead.
Go instead where there is no path and leave a trail.

- Ralph Waldo Emerson

Every spiritual journey begins when one asks the question: What is the first step? How do I flip the switch on the searchlight of my mind and access my internal compass that will guide me to a better understanding of my life and purpose?

Perhaps you have already begun your journey and you are wondering what the next step is. Contemplating some of the basic principles and premises underlying this book may assist you and propel you more rapidly on your spiritual adventure. Sometimes the first step is to review your life and see what is not working.

As a guide helping you along your path, I would like to share with you a little bit of my journey, my first steps during this lifetime. I call these "my truths" because they represent my experiences and points of view. This is what I have learned in the search for myself and ultimately in my search for God, my

God-power within. I had to begin by looking at what was not working in my life. The following is an example of where my search began.

I was raised Catholic and went to a Catholic school. Nuns had taught me all the rules, regulations, and concepts of the Catholic faith and Christian philosophy based on the teachings of Jesus, who I believe was a phenomenal master teacher and represents pure love. However, for me, many of the church doctrines never really made sense. The nuns always said it was only based on faith and I had to believe what they taught me. However, I could not fully grasp or accept that.

Somehow the teachings of Jesus about pure love never translated themselves the way they explained it. There seemed to be so many inconsistencies between the teachings of Jesus and the way people acted.

When I was very young, I accepted all the religious concepts because that is what my parents and other adults believed. Therefore, this is what I believed as well, even though I had my doubts deep down inside. I could not understand this confusion. Too many times I would see church representatives do things or hear them say things that were not as honorable as I thought they should be. These were my perceptions at the time.

For example, one of the things that continually disturbed me was the way the church officials always asked for money. They would publish in the church bulletin how much each family donated each year. That always made many families uncomfortable, including my own, because some people were richer and some were poorer. This made people feel unworthy and prompted them to donate more in order to compete with their neighbor, sometimes creating a hardship.

This money helped the church to continue operating, yet the methods seemed too pressured and intimidating, in my opinion. I felt, as a child, that the church (representing God) should act more honorably. Whether this was right or wrong, I can only decide for myself; nonetheless, these types of behaviors as well as some of the teachings shaped my thinking.

It seemed as though the church was teaching separation rather than love. I especially did not like the inferior role that women were forced to play in the major religions and in society. Again, this dynamic only created more separation rather than a true partnership between men and women.

As I grew older, I rejected Christianity altogether. The judgmental, angry Christian God was not the one I knew in my heart. Sending people to hell and babies to purgatory was not right in my heart and my mind, and I finally rejected this God altogether.

I became an atheist. As I grew older, I just wasn't sure and I became more of an agnostic. All through high school and in my twenties, I went back and forth between being an atheist (not believing in God) and an agnostic (not sure if there is a God, but not completely denying it).

In 1985 a friend gave me some information that turned my thinking into an entirely different direction, helping me get out of the religion "box" and look outside it for another perspective.

You will learn more about that in this book. I have spent the last several years searching for the answers for a God that fit me. I read every metaphysical and religious book I could get my hands on. Reading about all the different concepts and attributes of God, from different religious and spiritual points of view, helped me tremendously. It has been an amazing journey and I feel I have found my God that is loving and forgiving no matter what I do and is never apart from me. I am never alone.

This does not mean I don't take responsibility for myself. I always do and check with my ethics meter to discern my actions. I have done well, but I have also made many mistakes. My conclusion thus far has taught me that this journey took me from looking at the world and God as an external—meaning outside myself (the old man in the clouds scenario)—to the God who is within me, and part of my heart, and soul. This partnership is where my true power and my true self reside.

I tell you my story because I believe we all go through this search at some level. It was my lesson in this lifetime… like a test.

The question was: Can I be born on Planet Earth, this Third-Dimensional physical plane, forgetful of my past gifts, memories, and lessons, and find God again? Once we develop that inner, sacred relationship, can we learn to co-create with God to manifest a world that is Heaven on Earth? Not an easy task when religions keep telling us that we must look outside ourselves for the answers; and the priests, ministers, rabbis, etc., keep wanting us to come to them for our lessons.

I find this to be an abuse of power. Even though the clergy may have had good intentions to teach the word of God, it became more of an issue of using fear and control rather than love and guidance. This had much to do with my deep rejection of the church.

Somehow I sensed there was more of a loving, forgiving, expansive essence to God, not just the God the Bible or other religious texts described. I just knew there was more to it. For me, there was a God of unconditional love. Now that resonates with me.

It is very, very important that you understand that this is my path, my lessons, and my journey. Throughout this journey I used discernment, which means: "To come to know, to discriminate, to reveal insight and understanding or to judge something for yourself."

I will say it over and over again. Use discernment in all that you do. You are the judge, not your friends, family, or even God, who does not judge you. You are the only one who can make decisions for yourself.

In fact, I am not so sure I like the word *judgment*. It connotes too much negativity meaning rulings, verdicts, sentences, opinions about others and about self, so I prefer to use the word *discernment* as a way to reveal personal insight and understanding.

For example, when I read about a certain idea or concept, I think about it and ask myself, "Is this an idea that makes sense to me?" It is as if I bring the idea into my head and into my heart. I feel it, think about it, and then decide whether or not it makes sense. If it didn't, then I let it go. It was not right for me. It was not my truth.

As time went on, I learned to trust this intuition, this inner knowingness—to know something was simply right. This knowingness and trust in yourself is where I want to lead you. This is where our true power lies.

Follow along with me to understand some of the ideas and concepts that I have learned on my spiritual journey. Take in the ones that feel right; reject the ones that do not. Do not lose your sense of self as you follow my line of thinking. I am a teacher, "a student of the divine"[2] and a catalyst for you to search for your own ideas inside or outside the religious box.

I also believe there are truths in all of the religions. As Carolyn Myss[3] describes it, there are the chakras in the Hindu faith, the seven sacraments in the Christian faith, and the tree of life in the Jewish faith—all symbols of truth. The core of these teachings can help you to learn about yourself—the many layers of self.

However, I needed a broader perspective of these concepts than I received in the organized Christian religion. A lot of information was being left out of its teachings based on my personal experiences. So I began my search to look deeper. I was looking for my truth. I had this unquenchable thirst to know.

I do believe the Catholic Church gave me a good foundation to begin my search, but for me it was not enough. It may be all you need, and I encourage you to stay with what resonates with you.

It is also very important that you do not judge others wrongly for following along with their church, synagogue or faith of choice. They are not wrong; that is their path. It is right for them. It is their truth. We cannot judge them wrong because of their choice. All paths eventually lead back to God.

This is where being tolerant of other points of view comes into play. There is no right or wrong answer here. It is what is right for *you*. If you listen to your own heart and your own soul, you are on the right path for you. The churches can play a very important role in teaching people about values, about being open and tolerant of others' views, about teaching right from wrong, and about the many possibilities and mysteries of God.

However, in my opinion, I believe they have frequently swayed from their original purpose by attempting to shape people's thinking using manipulation, separation, and fear rather than offering choices in a loving, accepting way. The intolerance of other people's views and choices is probably where I also fell off the religious track. Some religions have a tendency to ram their teachings down people's throats, with a mentality that says, "If you are not one of us, then you are one of them and 'going to hell.'"

Separation and exclusion is not what religion should center on. Love, tolerance, and support of the other person's choice of path should remain the primary focus. As a Catholic child, I could never understand why my best friend was going to hell just because she was Lutheran. Again, that is where the church lost me.

I will probably anger some or get in trouble with others of the organized churches, but it is a risk I have to take. My purpose right now is to teach what I have learned on my path and to share it with those who are interested. If, at any time, while reading this book, something does not feel right to you, please use your own discernment and be empowered to put the book down. Give the book away and continue your search for something that resonates with you. I send you my love no matter what your choice. I honor you and can sense the true you.

As I look back at my process in finding my way and contemplate what I have written here, I can feel my old anger, confusion, and incredible judgment of the organized religious doctrines surfacing again. But I also feel I have grown tremendously over the years and have come to a place of forgiveness in all of this. I see now that it was me, and only me, who set up this scenario, which I call my lifetime contract to be born to these parents and siblings, go to Catholic school, and live the way I did.

It was a test that I planned this lifetime of opportunities before my birth to see if I could come back home to my true self. I have discovered it is where my true happiness, joy, appreciation, forgiveness, peace, and empowerment reside. It feels good.

Let's get started on your search to understand the true power of you, so you can join me in this place of peace. Maybe we can turn the whole planet into a place of peace and finally have Heaven on Earth. It is a vision I hold close to my heart.

CHAPTER 2

You Are a Co-Creator – A God in Training

We are not human beings having a spiritual experience.
We are spiritual beings having a human experience.

– Pierre Teilhard de Chardin

Right now on this earth, in our physical bodies, we are all "gods in training" co-creating with God. This is truly who we are.

That's a wild concept, isn't it? Contemplate that a moment before moving on. It is a lot to grasp at first—at least it was for me. [In my book I will refer to you and me as a "god," a co-creator, in lower case meaning "divinity" and not "idolatry." God capitalized is in reference to the Creator.]

We are all spirits, or gods in training, living in a physical, Third-Dimensional body, so we can explore, experiment, express, and experience everything within physical matter and emotion and share it with God.

When I first heard this, I felt so small and had to ask how could that be. It sounded so arrogant at first. Some religions would even say I was blasphemous.

The more I have learned about the "true me" and the "power" within me, the more I have come to accept this about myself.

In her books such as *Out on a Limb*[4], Shirley MacLaine provided the first introduction for me about this notion. In her search for self-discovery, this became her truth. I have since grown to a place within myself where this has become my truth as well. I encourage you to search for your truth and see if it fits. Keep an open mind and come along with me as we explore the notion that we are all gods.

For greater clarity, I refer to the Big God as "it" because the "unlimitedness," the "everness," and the "infiniteness" of the God source represents both male and female—it truly represents everything including the universal breath.

Why are we training as little gods to become Big Gods? It is my sense that we are aspects or pieces of the Big God. I am sure there are many other interpretations of this notion, but I needed to start in a place that my brain could comprehend. I had to start small.

So I began by imagining that there is one Big God and it is broken into many little pieces or particles. We are the little pieces—the little gods—and we are training to become Big Gods so we can co-create and assist the Big God in managing all the universes and omniverses.*

It is common scientific knowledge that your physical body is made up of millions of cells. Imagine your human body as the Big God made up of millions of little gods, which represent the cells in your body. The brain acts as the main director, organizer, and divine intelligence of the whole body.

That is why the Bible says we are the image of God, the body of Christ. Some assume the Bible meant that the Big God looks like an entire physical body. Possibly… but, for me, I imagine it differently, as I will explain later.

The cell concept is my way of visualizing the whole essence of God. We are all an aspect or piece of God—all One, all connected—with no separation. We perceive that we are separate, but we are not. Someone else may visualize this concept in a different way. That is an acceptable critique, because God is a mystery for all of us to figure out what resonates with our own individual soul.

You can also think of each physical cell as a complete body or the Big God.

Each cell is an efficient factory able to run all functions perfectly. It interacts with all the other cells around it to create a whole person. Each cell is separated by a cellular wall, yet all connected. They work best if connected to the whole, thereby increasing their efficiency and their purpose to being a whole person.

As little gods (cells), we function individually as a spark of the God light, yet we are connected to the whole body of the Big God so we can mutually fulfill our purposes and experience everything. That is what is meant by the expression: "*We are all one, with no separation.*"

We can take this one step further by describing each cell as an individual universe that also has a Big God and lots of little gods as mentioned above. The Big God represents the whole cell (universe) containing many organelles circulating within that could be referred to as the little gods.

We can keep this concept going smaller and smaller to find more Big Gods and little gods in atoms, quarks, etc., or we can imagine them as bigger and bigger, expanding it out to larger galaxies, universes, or omniverses in outer space—all having Big Gods and little gods in training embodying a supreme order and intelligence functioning within the divine plan.

Just let your imagination run wild with no limits or expectations and keep imagining how many designs and aspects of God you can come up with!

Back to visualizing our physical human body again at the cellular level… now try to understand that we have an emotional component to this body in the form of blood and other fluids that work between each of the cells. I see them as emotion or the "universal glue"[5] that adheres the cells together functioning along with the brain, which is the central computer.

This glue of love, flowing between each of our cells, personifies the emotion that connects us to each other and to the Big God. Along with love, exist the vibrations of sound, movement, and the rainbow of colors. If you hold a prism up to the sun, you will see a rainbow of light reflected back to you on the wall. These are your true rainbow colors, or your soul colors, wrapped in love.

We see in each other this divine rainbow of light. We see this light with our inside "soul" eyes rather than our outside "physical" eyes. We feel this love with our divine heart, knowing that this glue called *love* connects us together. When the Big God said, "Let there be light," we were created within this divine matrix of love. Within love is the vibration of movement. To have movement, we need some kind of friction, the rubbing together of two elements, which produces a spark of movement. This spark began all of creation giving birth to light as well as dark. This is known as duality, (also referred to as karma).*

We live many lifetimes to master duality and achieve oneness. This is commonly known as reincarnation,* which means the rebirth of the soul into a new body. Imagine your physical body as the car you drive around in this lifetime and that you will drive around in yet another new car, or a new physical body, in the next lifetime. However, your "engine," which is your spiritual heart and soul (not your physical heart), remains the same and with you every lifetime, along with all the memories.

You store these memories and experiences in what is called the Akashic Records* in the spiritual realms. These are your private, personal records of all your lives and you are the only one who can scrutinize them. You review your records after each lifetime to see what you have learned and then you set up a new contract with yourself, laying out the lessons you plan to learn in your next life.

That is the true meaning of "Judgment Day." Each time you are born into your new car (physical body), you forget about all the other lifetimes. This forgetfulness is referred to as "being veiled" but, at a very deep level, you bring with you some of those past-life memories. It helps make each life easier because, as time goes on, you become a much wiser soul.

You do not have to relearn lessons. But you do have to learn the things you don't seem to master. If you are stuck on some lesson, you will have it appear over and over again in your current lifetime as well as in future lifetimes until you thoroughly understand it. There is no judgment, or failure, or "hell" if you do not learn your lesson—only new opportunities to learn it until you figure it out.

Then that lesson goes into your soul bank account or spiritual Akashic Records and you say to yourself, "I have learned this lesson, so now I am ready to accept my new assignments." Isn't it grand? You are always growing, loving, changing, and learning, making conscious choices leading to your grand soul purpose, which is co-creating with God.

Co-creating is accomplished with your thoughts combined with the powerful emotion of appreciation. You team up with God through your thoughts and create what you want in to your life and what God wants to create with you. Wow! What a concept.

Imagine that we all began as a thought in the Big God's infinite mind. We first began as emptiness or the void, and then moved into the thought. From that thought sprang the light. From the light came color, blossoming into the thirteen rays of creation, which on the earth plane is manifested as the colors of the rainbow. From color came the dimensions. From there came matter and anti-matter.

A long, long time ago, we were seated with the breath of the Big God. Some of us decided we didn't want to exist within the void anymore, because we wanted to create and utilize our free will and free choice on our own. Some call this the "fall from grace," or the creation and expansion of darkness or negativity.

In this fall, or perceived separation, we forgot we were gods. Many of us having forgotten who we are, live on this earth currently. We are in the "school called Planet Earth"[6] (a phrase coined by Dr. James Martin Peebles), so we can remember who we are, learn our lessons, release karma, self-forgiveness for our fall from grace, fulfill our contracts of experiencing light and darkness and return to the breath and light of the God Source again.

Many of you are already awakened or conscious enough to know whom you are at a soul level and what your gifts are. Some of you are still asleep (or unconscious, spiritually speaking), and completely forgetful of your gifts. We all awaken to our soul-self eventually, and you will too.

You are not to be judged. You are not doing anything wrong. You just haven't awakened to your soul purpose yet. For those of you who are awakening, this book will assist you in understanding who you are and why you are *different* from others. I want you to have confidence in knowing you are different and not be afraid or turn away from your spiritual gifts.

You are not crazy or possessed. You are awake. You know things beyond the five senses. You are moving beyond the physical body of matter and becoming a crystalline/etheric/light body. More children being born today are awake and the sleeping ones do not know what to do with all of them.

I have just introduced a huge number of concepts and possibilities. It is very important that you begin to see the panoramic view in all of this and connect it to your life. You may need to reread the chapter to comprehend the full magnitude of these concepts.

Use your imagination, similar to what I just visualized, and design a picture of what God looks and feels like to you. It may be different from mine. No matter what you imagine there is no wrong answer. Now expand that picture to include creating something with your thoughts. How do you do that?

Below is an example of how to create with thought, individually and collectively. You already do it every day. Taking the leap to conscious awareness of how powerful your thoughts can be will awaken the "wow" inside of you. You are a co-creator with God.

The power of being a co-creator is very simple once you understand the larger, spiritual perspective, and become aware of its simplicity and potency.

As explained above, we are all little "gods-in-training" experiencing physical matter and designing and manifesting things and emotions all the time, allied with the Big God. Therefore, we are co-creators or partners in the process.

Visualize that as you move your hand to create something, imagine God's hand on top of yours, creating and experiencing with you, and working together as a team.

For example, the next time you eat breakfast and you read the cereal box, think about the number of co-creators who were consciously aware of their purpose and then produced that cereal and its packaging. It is a simple concept, but you get the idea.

Farmers harvested the grains and others ran the storage facilities for it. Trains and trucks delivered the grain to the bakers who made the dough and shaped all the little cereal flakes. Next in line came the box designers: the timber man who cut the trees for the paper and the box maker who made the tree pulp into cardboard and shaped the cereal box.

Include the artist who drew all the graphics and pictures for the boxes and the writer who created all the information about the cereal's great flavor and nutritional value. Then consider all the people in the warehouses—packing, moving, and shipping all these cereal flakes in boxes to the grocery store.

Finally, you shop in the grocery store and buy this box of cereal. There you are right now eating your cereal and staring at the cereal box that all those little gods in training made.

It All Begins with a Thought!

The thought was "I am hungry." How can we all work together and make a box of cereal so everyone can share the farmer's grains? Surely we cannot forget that nature had a hand in all of this as well.

Nature expresses herself as a co-creator and is a part of God too. Wisdom thrives in that seed of grain to produce wheat. Somewhere along the line, God and all the co-creators invented nature.

Again, it all started with a thought. God invites our assistance in all of creation—from corn flakes to universes—and encompasses more than just light, air or a man in the clouds. It expresses everywhere, but it prefers to make it a team effort. God needs our conscious assistance and consensus to create movement in the physical worlds.

Creating something simple like a cereal box of corn flakes demonstrates God in action. Bringing in our collective creations refines God's plan. So whether you choose to become a leader of a country or work in that factory making corn flakes, you are exactly where you are supposed to be—co-creating with God.

It Is Fulfilled with Appreciation!

There is one more element to this that you should consider. Yes, we are all co-creators. But another part of being a co-creator is having appreciation for all that you and God create.

Sit in that chair and eat your cereal and really appreciate the process of creating a box of corn flakes. This may sound silly. But I use a simple example, such as creating cereal, to bring the notion of co-creation down to a practical level.

Thus, when you communicate the emotions of love, gratitude and appreciation, this expression opens and fills your heart further, and brings you closer to God. You can also feel that you are one with the collective who made that cereal. You all participated in making it using your communal thought. When you can go through your life consciously aware of your creations and truly appreciate them, it moves you into a more balanced, peaceful, and joyful state. Everyday, I appreciate and enjoy the food on my table, as many people on our planet go hungry or have never even seen a cereal box. I appreciate all that I am blessed with in my life.

The wild and wonderful concept that I am a spiritual being expressing myself as a co-creator with God is amazing to me. Mastering this concept truly accentuates and highlights the importance of what we do every day in our lives. Being consciously present in every moment, by enjoying eating our corn flakes or appreciating the chair we sit on, really brings in a new meaning to our everyday existence. It will change your whole perspective as you embrace the practicality of spirituality. Be the conscious observer and co-creator and watch what happens.

Go forth this day and go about your "Father's/Mother's" business.

– Orpheus Phylos,* a spiritual teacher, author, and channel for Archangel Michael

CHAPTER 3

What If God Is a Spiral?

Blessed are they that have not seen and have believed.

– John 20:29

Who is this Big God anyway? What does this Big God some call "source" or "radiant one" look like? To whom do I pray? What is his/her/its purpose?

These are all questions people have asked for eons of time. The different world religions have come up with various names and interpretations. Some call it God, Allah, Source, the Void, the Radiant One, YHVH, Jesus, the Breath, Creator, Everness, Universal Mind, or the God of Oneness. It has many names and images.

I believe the world religions have part of the information but not all. There are so many mysteries that we just don't understand yet or have forgotten. (I know that I am still remembering and am sure my information just barely scratches the surface.)

It is very important that you understand this, and, as noted earlier, that I am not here to judge anyone's path. If the information of the religion of your choice fulfills you, then you have found your path. I truly honor you for your choices.

However, if you are interested or maybe just curious about another more expansive point of view, I ask you to look further. Dig deeper inside yourself. If it feels as though your soul hungers for something more, then pursue your search within to define your truth.

Where is your source, your God, and what does he/she/it look, feel, and sound like? To whom do you pray?

Let's use our imaginations and explore what God looks like. That is what I do all the time. I often wonder what God actually looks like since, in my opinion, the divine doesn't resemble me in my physical human form.

The Bible says we are created in God's image. We have always assumed it meant a human form. Some even think of God as a male figure—an old bearded guy up in the clouds watching over us. That might be only one aspect of God, since it has been created in someone's mind in that form. That is appropriate too, because it is his or her truth.

What shapes might embody the attributes of God? What if God expresses as a spiral, for example, that comprises our DNA? (DNA exists within the cells of our physical body and contains our genetic blueprint.) Perhaps several different geometric shapes, such as a triangle, circle, or a square, symbolize aspects of God, and each has its own special vibratory rate or tone.

Many of our ancient cultures drew geometric shapes on cave walls, such as the spiral in the Native American culture. We see the triangle in the pyramids of ancient Egypt. We see circles everywhere—in the sun, the moon, and the stars.

Some speculate that geometry is actually an ancient language of vibration and musical tones. We use our five senses to see the shapes, feel, and even taste the vibrations and hear the musical tones.

The dodecahedron symbol* is a 12-sided polyhedron with pentagonal faces. Perhaps the shape of a dodecahedron embodies the traits of God? Maybe, but we will never know for sure. Even a dodecahedron expresses itself with limiting borders. In actuality, God's expressions signify limitless infinity without edges or boundaries.

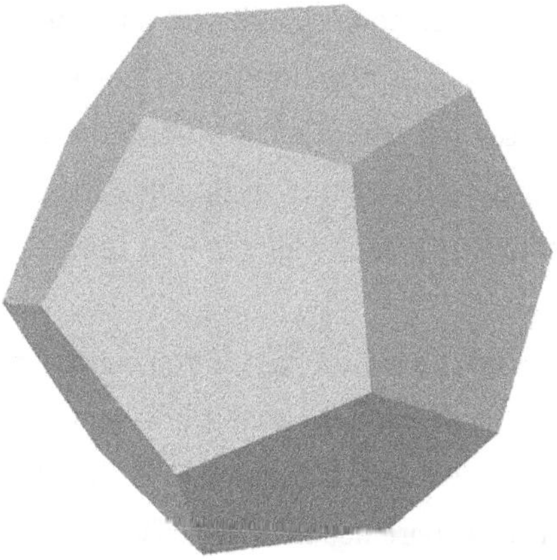

We can see all the geometric shapes in nature. Think of these as God's reflections. God is demonstrating and communicating about itself all the time and every day through nature, showing us how it looks if we take the time to sense how it feels and what it sounds like. Notice when we commune with nature, we feel comfort, peace, contentment and even love.

These are some possibilities of how God may look. Begin to visualize what God may look like to you in whatever forms you wish. Just know that it is hard to imagine "unlimitedness." If necessary, it is acceptable to give God a shape or face in your mind; the God Source will not object a bit. The God image I described above as a body—as a Big God and little gods—still has a boundary or edge. Actually, there is no boundary, only "unlimitedness." However, for clarity, we had to start somewhere.

Another important thing about God is how God expresses. What if God is not a geometric symbol at all, but pure emotion? What if God represents the absolute purest attributes of unconditional love?

The emotion of God cannot be easily expressed in words; you must experience it yourself. In my meditations, I have felt such incredible, deep, emotional, unconditional love—way beyond the love you feel for yourself, your friends, your family, and even the most important love of your life. It exemplifies so much more than that. It fills you up more fully than you can ever imagine.

People who have had out-of-body experiences can share more details about this unconditional love. Dannion Brinkley[7], an author who has had out-of-body/near-death experiences and who has come back to share his understanding of death, offers a compelling account of feeling this love, and how it changed his life to live without fear. His book will give you his insight into this place and feeling.

This emotion of love that God has for you is immense and unconditional. Despite what you do or say, and no matter how bad or evil you think you are, God will still love you without conditions or expectations and forgive you. I hope someday you can experience this immense love for yourself.

The best way to access it is to go into a meditative state and ask your higher self,* your spiritual guides, teachers, and God to help you experience it. I will share more details about meditation later. In the meantime, you can begin by practicing this simple meditation.

Get comfortable, close your eyes and take a few deep breaths. In your mind, say hello to your higher self (your soul-self) and listen for the answer. You may get a hello back. What fun! Take a few more breaths and request your higher self or spiritual guides to send you the vibratory sensation of unconditional love. Take a few more, deep, slow breaths and wait for the blissful feeling of love, peace and joy. When I do this exercise, I frequently sense a smile on my face, and even a few tears, as I relish the loving emotion as it fills me completely.

You may not feel or hear anything at all, at first, because your higher self will only let you experience what you are ready for. You are always protected and guided to experience what you are capable of learning at the present moment. Sometimes these things can take a lifetime or two in order to achieve your aspirations. The actual intent of asking to experience it will make it happen eventually. Your spiritual guides and teachers will find a way for you to experience this unconditional love at just the right moment.

Another good book for exploring the different levels of creation is *Worlds Beyond Death* by Dr. Grant H. Pealer.[8] He has one of the most amazing explanations of other dimensions and parts of God that I have ever read. It is definitely a huge "what if" question to explore his interpretation of the other worlds. If you are new to your spiritual quest, consider adding this book to your reading list. You will know when you are ready to explore the many worlds beyond our present reality.

Let me expand once more on this concept of our God source and take it a bit further. Maybe God is not a shape or emotion at all, but a vibration of thought, which can be expressed as words, colors, movement or even sound as in the tones of a song.[9] Think about that one!

It is said that God began creating in the void, a womb of potentiality, receptivity, and stillness. Within this birthplace, God decided to manifest thought. From there, light came into being. This beautiful light is comprised of millions of colors and vibrations.

The rainbow in the sky is an example of some of the vibratory colors we can see with our naked eye. These have been referred to as the Thirteen Rainbow Rays of Creation. Many other colors exist in different planes of existence and universes that remain invisible to us.

Isn't it interesting that children always draw pictures with rainbows in them? Even at a young age, on an unconscious level, we remember the rainbow of light. We could probably see other colors in our mind but did not have those colors in our crayon box.

After the Source God created thought, light, and the rainbow rays, it created unconditional love. This is the "universal glue" that holds everything together. From there, it created matter and anti-matter.

But, wait; all of this had to move around, so then it created movement. Perhaps the geometric shapes of the spiral, circle or triangle, for example, evolved as one of the forces to move things around. Next, free will manifested as a universal law. From there, God created balance, which is the "constant alignment of all creation from the source." Some refer to this as karma at the physical level.

The four Laws of the Universe are Love, Light, Free Will and Balance.[10] As God created, it also manifested what is called the Triad of Energy:* intent, data, and expression.[11] Intent equates to the spiritual blueprint, data to the mental blueprint and expression to the emotional blueprint. The final stage creates the manifestation of physical movement into matter, represented by our physical body, or physical movement into matter within the alignment between spirit, data, and expression.

To summarize these concepts, the four universal laws* are:

1. "Light: First law of the universe. The active expression of the Source, throughout all creation. This is also an expression of the masculine principle.
2. Love: Second law of the universe. The passive expression of the Source throughout all of creation. Love is the universal glue that holds all of creation together. This is also an expression of the feminine principle.
3. Free Will: Third law of the universe. Free will represents expansion constantly directed from the Source but constantly providing outward movement.
4. Balance: Fourth law of the universe. The constant alignment of all creation from the Source. Some refer to it as karma (cause and effect) at the physical level.

And these are the three Triads of Energy—that brought forth the creation of the physical and non-physical levels of the universe:

1. Intent – spiritual blueprint
2. Data – mental blueprint
3. Expression – emotional blueprint"[12]

Therefore, by incorporating intent, data, and expression with the four laws of the universe—love, light, free will, and balance—we align all our bodies (physical, emotional, mental, and spiritual) to a position of good health and well-being that helps us take control of our life and realize our full potential.

All of these represent levels of vibration. To manifest matter, the vibratory rate must become denser—a compactness and hardness of the vibrations. The cells in our bodies constitute energy, which incorporates the movement of vibration.

The bodies we chose express themselves in many types, shapes and sizes. We perceive the human form, the animal form, insects, fish, germs, viruses, bacteria, and many other types of cells on Planet Earth that we cannot see with the naked eye. We can view some of them through the microscope.

Just because we cannot perceive them does not mean they do not exist. For all we know, there might be very strange-looking beings of all shapes and sizes living on other planets. We just have not met them yet.

All of this energy stirs within you. The physical cells, your emotions, and your mental data are expressions of your true spiritual self. This represents your spiritual intent, meaning that you dwell within as a spiritual body, a part of God, expressing itself in the physical form.

Therefore, your universe really exists within yourself. God is actually *within you*, and that is where you need to look, feel, think, listen, and even pray.

Now back to discussing that spiral. All of this manifestation came from God as thought and spirals down from there. So perhaps God is not actually the spiral, but its footprint around the universes, omniverses, and a variety of many dimensions.

It is everywhere. What does a spiral signify, after all? It means "to continuously spread and increase, to wind or coil around a center axis and usually getting closer to or farther away from it." Hmmm…

Right now, our perception senses a distance from that central axis. At least it seems that way. However, that is the illusion of separation. God is within you and never far away. You are always loved and always cared for.

We have chosen for the moment to manifest physical bodies to explore this earth school to learn a set of lessons. This is where our intent, our free will, free choice and our karma (balance) gets to play itself out, so have fun. You can explore your inner world and find your God within.

When you pray to your God within, what vision will you hold in your mind's eye? Perhaps you feel comfortable seeing a shape like a spiral, or you simply feel the love, or you hear god in a song. Maybe you see, hear and feel God in all of these.

We all have our own individual vision of God. It is whatever you manifest it to be. Imagine your *face of God* to be whatever you like. Pray to that face. If you sense God is outside of yourself, see if you can visualize God moving within you. Feel the love and joy of God within you. It feels so good.

Let's pause for a moment here to explore our inner worlds and experience finding our God Source within. Here is a mediation tool you can use to feel the sensation of God:

Listen – Begin to focus on your breath. Deeply inhale and slowly exhale, tuning in for the sound the air makes as it gently flows through your nose and lungs. Repeat several times as you concentrate on the present. Notice how the body and mind respond in your relaxed and peaceful God moment. If you quietly listen, you may hear a whisper from God, your higher self or your spiritual guides.

Look – Observe the pause, the space between the breaths, as some perceive God residing in that in-between space. When you inhale, consciously hold your breath for a moment and look for the still point and the silence that resides there. Then slowly exhale, basking in your newly discovered blissful moment. Notice how your breath moves slower and slower, allowing for a longer pause between breaths.

Feel – Relax and feel your body lose its tensions of the day. Continue to stay with the immediacy of your breath. Allow yourself to go deeper within your breath and your being. Your mind may wonder off to a stressful place in your body. Focus there and fully feel it for a moment, relax into it, and slowly move back to feeling and listening to your breath. Inhale deeply; notice the pause; exhale–all in one smooth, gentle rhythm. Next, when feeling complete with the breath exercise, gradually place your fingertips on your wrist and feel your pulse—tuning in to your heartbeat while connecting with the heartbeat of God.[13] Notice the thumping drumbeat of the pulse. Is it slow or fast? Continue to hold the wrist as you become aware of your whole body vibrating into a transcending rhythm and, at times, even connecting to the heartbeat of the earth. Immerse yourself in the bliss of the moment. This is one of many ways to perceive God within your being.

See how simple and easy that was? Do you have a better sense of God within? If not, don't worry; stay with me here and just keep reading. If it doesn't work for you at first, it will later as we learn more principles and do some more exercises together.

There are unlimited, hallowed names, faces, visions and sensations of God. Some people may envision their God with no name or face. My vision may resonate with me, but maybe not with you. You have your own vision. Both are right as both come from our heart and from our God within. Why do I ask you to ponder your vision of God in any shape or size? I am encouraging you to think outside your current "box." As you widen your vision of God, you expand the truth of whom you are, leading to your rightful place of empowerment. "How do you like them apples"?[14]

You are such beautiful spirits. It is through your prayers, spoken, silent, willing, surrendering, that you learn about yourself. Every prayer is for you. Every prayer is to your spirit that you may understand God within self: to give Him acknowledgment, to allow for Him to rise to the surface of your being, to feel the peace and the comfort and the strength that comes with this knowing.

– Dr. James Martin Peebles as channeled through Summer Bacon work they do not, it will [illegible] we [illegible] more [illegible] and [illegible] more everlasting [illegible].

There are hundreds of hallowed names [illegible] of God. Some people may [illegible] their God [illegible] with no [illegible] vision [illegible] with major [illegible] may be [illegible] with you [illegible] have your [illegible] both are [illegible] from our heart and [illegible] of God [illegible]. When we look [illegible] to [illegible] your vision of God in [illegible] I am encouraging you to think outside your current "box." As you [illegible] your vision of God, you expand the truth of [illegible] you are [illegible] to [illegible] place of [illegible] [illegible] life [illegible] apples.

[illegible] surrounding [illegible] your [illegible] prayer [illegible] Every prayer [illegible] your spirit [illegible] you [illegible] understand God within [illegible] [illegible] fulfillment [illegible] [illegible] [illegible] [illegible] and [illegible] with the [illegible]

[illegible]
[illegible]

CHAPTER 4

Love Yourself

To love oneself is the beginning of a life-long romance.

– Oscar Wilde

To me love is like the wind. I can feel it on my face and sometimes hear the wind as it rustles through the leaves. But I can't see it; I can only feel it. Just because I cannot see it does not mean it is not there.

God is similar to the wind and touches you much the same way. Acknowledge that God is within you as you feel the magnification of its power source, which in turn becomes your power source.

God reaches you through your emotion. It is God's connection to you through your spiritual heart that carries you to the heart of the divine. Acknowledge that this feeling of love flourishes within you.

Take a moment to think of someone you love. Take a few deep breaths, then close your eyes and explore what feelings come to you.

You feel good about that person. Perhaps that person is your father. When your memories of him drift into your mind, he makes you smile. You see his good traits and bad, but you love him anyway. You have a feeling of affection for this person. You get a sense of him in your heart. You feel it in your heart or chest area like a bubbly, warm feeling. Sometimes you feel it in your solar plexus area, which is around or above your belly button. Can you acknowledge giving your love to him unconditionally? Can you receive his love in return unconditionally?

Think of how you feel toward your pet. You love this creature. Your pet loves you back unconditionally. You know this because you can feel it. Animals innately know how to love unconditionally.

Loving unconditionally means you love that person or pet without any preconceived expectations of how they should be or should behave. They are just being who they are, true to themselves, and, in return, do not judge you or expect you to behave a certain way.

They forgive you immediately if, for some reason, you are having a bad day and take it out on them. If that happens, when you feel better, you just go to that person or your pet and hug them and say you are sorry. They forgive you and forget all about it and love you no matter what.

You love your husband or wife, mother and father, your brothers and sisters, grandmas and grandpas, aunts and uncles, cousins, friends—everyone in your life. Now imagine how large God's love is for you--possibly as expansive and unlimited as the sky with no expectations. That "unlimitedness" portrays the potential of unconditional love.

No matter what you do, God will always love you and be there for you. Many times you will forget that God dwells within and you may not feel God around you—an illusion of separation. You can also imagine that God encompasses everything and exists everywhere.

Imagine infinity if you can. Visualize the sky, a tree, a rock, even the chair you sit on, and contemplate the possibility that God exists in each of those places and more. God is embodied in each of those objects and even the space in between. Acknowledge that God dwells within you.

The best way to feel God's love is to find a place within yourself where you feel grateful for what you have. Gratitude expresses the power of God's inner presence in a wonderful way. This comes to the most important part of all, where you must love yourself first before anything else. You may not be able to figure out this one at first, but I share this now so you can work toward it as a goal.

Not everyone arrives on Planet Earth knowing how to love. Sometimes our parents don't know how to love themselves, so they don't know how to teach it to you. Somewhere, along their journey, they have forgotten how to love.

Find a place within yourself where you feel this love and accept that they are doing the best they can with what they know. Life unfolds as a journey in which we each encounter certain lessons. Maybe you take on the role as the teacher for your wife, husband or parents to teach them how to love—to love themselves first, and then to love you. It expands as a circle of reciprocal energy. Loving yourself first is a gift of compassion, not an act of selfishness. When you love yourself first, then you are truly able to love others.

Without *love of self,* your gift box would be empty. When you give a gift to someone, you first have a feeling you want to share something. You put that feeling into your "love" gift box and then give it to your mom, for example. She receives your gift, and with it comes your feeling of love, but you needed to have that love for yourself first in order to share it with your mom. It becomes this "give and receive" gesture that creates the circle of reciprocated love energy.

Think of love energy as movement. This movement of love represents God in action. Creating the movement of love all around the earth, the solar system, the galaxy, the universe, demonstrates God's purpose. To love yourself manifests your purpose. If you don't know how to do it yet—well, learning to love yourself first represents one of your aspirations and purpose in this lifetime.

God will wait for you to learn your lesson of self-love. God will never stop loving you while it waits. In fact, it will send all kinds of spiritual angels, guides, and teachers to assist you in learning self-love. Everyone will eventually learn this lesson—pacing themselves for their highest good and always without any judgment, punishment or anger.

To feel love and to give and receive love is a complex and profound topic. Love of self becomes the starting point in understanding and experiencing this complexity. Too many times in our lives we seem to love another much easier than ourselves. Sometimes we even love too much when we encroach on others' lives by engulfing them in our love, but it ends up being love with conditions and expectations.

Learning to love ourselves first becomes our primary lesson in this lifetime. Our many relationships and interactions with others are our best teachers. Some say love becomes our only lesson.

When you truly learn to balance the *giving and receiving* of the love cycle, you have discovered the depth of your power, but it all starts with you expressing love first. Can you ride on the wings of the wind and passionately express your power of love? Happiness and joy are your rewards.

CHAPTER 5

The Power of Choice

Synchronicity is an ever-present reality for those who have eyes to see it..

– Carl Jung

You make many choices in your life—ones that lead you down a certain path or direction. If you choose to take a certain job or go to a certain school, for example, it will guide you to meet certain people and develop relationships with them. Some of these relationships will be good ones and others very challenging. Usually, the most difficult relationships will be your greatest teachers.

When you are young, you tend to blame others for your mistakes. It will help you in life to understand that "through your own choices and perceptions, you do indeed create your own reality."[15] You have to take responsibility for these choices and for the individuals you meet. Challenging people hold a mirror before you, so to speak, so you can see for yourself what you need to learn. They serve as catalysts to help you embrace that lesson through them. What a gift they have to offer you!

This process works both ways in that you serve as teachers for each other, reminding one another that you are both gods in training. It is your light and your energy that they really see. Many times in these relationships, the universal laws of *give and receive* as well as *action and reaction*, frequently referred to as karma, become involved.

Karma activates a cause-and-effect principle through which you do one thing to someone and then later the same or similar act reappears and comes back to you—sometimes tenfold. If you give out "good" it returns to you as good. If you put forth "bad," it too will reverberate back to you as "bad." To arrive at a point where the action and reaction are complete, you reach a place of equilibrium or balance. Here, love is able to flow freely without blockages. Once you learn this, you will become more sensitive on how you treat other people. You have the power to choose how to act and react. This is an extremely important concept to understand and I will explain more about it in the next chapter.

The power of one's choices is also the universal law of "free will and free choice." It profoundly shapes your life. For example, when I review my current lifetime and look at the moment I had two job offers; I noticed that each one could lead to different pathways of opportunity. Each came with new relationships and new experiences I needed to learn about.

As I look back on my final choice, I become aware how my life would have been different had I chosen the other option. The decision I made was not a good one. Little did I know at the time, how perfectly my daily journey was synchronized with my life's contract, and how I was absolutely in the right place at the right time to learn what I needed to learn becoming the person I am today.

When I look back at the so-called wrong decision, I remember my mind starting to engage in what I call the "babbling thoughts," or the regrets, telling myself I should have done this, or I should have done that, and I could have done it this way. The "shoulds" and "coulds" start rambling and repeating their mantras over and over in my head.

I eventually learned that this type of negative thinking and self-doubt talk became very destructive behavior and challenged me to shift my thoughts. Even though it was not an easy pattern to change, I finally figured out it represented my personality or ego mind chattering and getting in the way rather than the productive thoughts of my higher mind.

If you catch yourself doing this, try to stop this babble in your head. It is both counter-productive and frustrating. Remind yourself to step back and see the broader horizon of God's grand plan for you. It is your grand plan too. You both decided what lessons you would learn in this lifetime. You made a contract with God and yourself before you were born. You are exactly where you need to be. There are no mistakes.

Take a closer look and examine the process of making a choice. At first, you evaluate your options, struggling between two choices. Should I go right or left? You stall and reach a standstill, often stuck in a mind-spinning whirlwind unsure what to do. Then comes the moment when you decide, "Oh, I will go right since that will offer me more opportunities."

Finally, you move forward, feeling confident in your decision, creating movement and the change in your life that you seek. Notice the key word here is *movement,* as you instantly begin to flow from the stuck place to one of mobility.

I look back at my life now and see all the synchronistic miracles that have happened because of my choices. I still cringe sometimes when I recall my "so-called" mistakes. But I now know all was in the right order. They were not mistakes. The situations, all the people I met, the challenges I faced, and the things I did not do as well as I should have, were all perfect and all in right order according to my contract.

Now I feel grateful for what I have experienced. They were my best teachers. I can feel love for myself and gratitude for those special relationships, situations, and dramas I experienced with them.

This is the shift in thinking that needs to occur—the grand test. If you don't pass it the first time, you, God, your higher self, and your angel guides will find another opportunity for you to do so. Another new school or job with new relationships will come into your life with the same lessons, but only the names and faces will change.

The challenge is the same. There is no judgment if you don't pass the test the first time, or the second time, or the third. There is only love, understanding, and patience—only a gentle push and guidance to assist you on your own path to fulfill your lifetime contract. You will eventually achieve your goals.

Think of God as a father/mother. Moms and dads teach their children to do the right things and to be the best they can be and to live a happy life. They only guide them from a place of love.

Your parents always love YOU, no matter what you do. It is only your behavior or action that might need a correction. They may say (from the heart) that they love you no matter what, but right now your behavior is unacceptable. You make the choice to take responsibility for this action and turn it into correct action. (Some parents are better at this than others. Parents are learning and managing the best they can.)

Our parents participate in their lesson plans right along with us. Know that children do not come with an instruction manual. And know this: God participates right along with you and me, prompting each of us to learn what is important at this time in our journey called life. So choose to love yourself and others unconditionally, without judgment. Love yourself, forgive yourself, and listen to your own heart, for it will guide you and offer many choices along the way, creating the movement, shifts, and changes you seek. Notice and respect the power of your choices.

Love is the ultimate teacher. It is God's voice. There are no mistakes. You are exactly where you are supposed to be. "Enjoy the journey to your own heart…."[16]

CHAPTER 6

The Power of Self-Responsibility, with a Dash of Ethics, Compassion, Forgiveness, and a Twist of Karma

If you want others to be happy, practice compassion.
If you want to be happy, practice compassion.

– Dalai Lama

The twists and turns of self-responsibility enable you to take charge and direct your thoughts and actions every day, leading to a happier and more successful journey.

You are a designer co-creating with God, choosing and shaping your life with what you will consciously think, feel, say, and do, as well as how you will respond. Contemplate the power you have to choose this perspective, rather than being a bystander and letting life just happen to you.

No one can really demonstrate this potential to you. Your parents tried to teach you responsibility by helping you learn how to manage your life, get to school on time, manage your bedtime, and take your meals—all the external things you do in your daily life. Your parents taught you these habits so you could grow up to be a responsible adult.

You can easily learn to take care of your physical needs and wants, but self-responsibility goes far deeper than that. It is an inner-directive (an ethics meter) that comes from deep inside your conscious and unconscious mind. It is the message in your head that says, "I can do 'this' for me, without hurting someone. I love me so much and I love others so much that I will do the right thing to the best of my ability. I will conduct my behaviors in an ethical manner because it is the responsible and right thing to do. I am that important." It means you love yourself, care about yourself and, as a result, care for others without an agenda. There are no conditions for your actions. You feel compassion, which means you have a sympathetic emotion. You acknowledge and respond to someone or something, yet compassion means you also understand how someone else absorbs and responds to emotion. You take responsibility for these actions.

It is a huge challenge to learn about yourself as you mature but, as time goes on, you become more and more comfortable with yourself. You learn who you are. The older you are and the more experiences you undergo, the easier it becomes. The tricky part begins when you start experiencing relationships with others.

For example, you eventually find a comfort zone with yourself, but realize that person in front of you has both lessons to teach and to learn. You act as teachers for each other. Your brother or sister is a teacher; your mom and dad are huge teachers—and not just when you are a kid.

Your best friend is a teacher and later, if you marry, your spouse or partner will serve as your teacher. Even your children will be there for you as a teacher to show you the lessons you need to learn. You both agreed to interchange the student/teacher roles. Many times, these interactions open the door for positive and negative actions and reactions creating a karmic situation.

Karma is the interaction of the positive and negative energies. Here is one basic example of negative karma: You act mean to someone in this lifetime, and that person reciprocates meanness to you in the next lifetime. You each create, transform, and transmute the emotional experience and the response of meanness resulting in a balanced karma or place of neutrality, thereby healing and releasing this old wound.

You both agreed and facilitated the healing process for each other to experience and understand the dark, lower vibrations of meanness. You perceived the sensation and felt what it was like to give meanness or receive meanness, thereby gaining insight, maturity and wisdom on this particular misguided behavior, and hopefully, have no need to repeat the experience again.

While karma represents a very complex process, it's important to understand the give and receive, and ultimately the balance that happens with all cause-and-effect actions and reactions.

Here is a possible, negative karmic scenario you may have to deal with some time while in college or at work.

For example, you have a classmate or co-worker who tells a lie about you to your other friends. You find out about it and you get angry. What do you do about it? How do you respond? That is the problem, as well as the test for you to handle and learn a particular lesson.

Perhaps, in this instance, your lesson is to speak your truth. You feel the emotions of anger, hurt, and sadness due to the fact that someone would do this to you. Your first reaction may be to go home and cry. This is a normal reaction and you may need to experience it to release this emotion of hurt out of your body. Trust and feel your emotions.

Next, anger sets in. Now you may want to get even or hurt them too, by following their actions and spreading a lie about them. You could go talk to other people and gossip about this person. You may need to do all of these things so you learn about the karmic relationship of cause and effect.

But, in the end, hopefully you will realize that the best course of action is to approach the lying person for a conversation. Ask the individual why he or she said this lie about you and whether he or she had the incorrect information. Inform the person that you would like him or her to stop saying these things. It hurts you and makes you feel uncomfortable.

You have now made the conscious choice to speak your truth. You are facing this person, telling him or her your truth. You now act as teachers for each other. Your classmate or co-worker is teaching you how to make the right choice to speak your truth and you are teaching your classmate or co-worker how to behave in a more loving, ethical manner without lying.

You take responsibility for your actions by remaining true to yourself and speaking your mind honestly. Your friend also has the choice to take responsibility for his or her actions.

If the individual does not stop the inappropriate behavior, **it is not your responsibility.** Just say, "Oh well, he or she is choosing wrong behavior here and I can only be responsible for me but not for others." Show compassion for the other person and love him or her anyway because we are all connected as *one,* and then just let it go.

With this type of thinking, you have released the negative karma that could have developed between each of you. You both could have chosen to spread several lies about each other until you both became enemies. You would continue to set up situations like this over and over again, lifetime after lifetime, until you get it, which is your lesson of self-responsibility for your actions.

As you go through life, you will experience many interactions with people. Just know they are your teachers–with no inappropriate behaviors, only lessons. Prior to your birth, part of your contract involved setting up a meeting with this person at a specific time and place, to assess and determine if a particular lesson had been mastered. If not, you will meet each other repeatedly, in this lifetime or the next, as mentioned before, until you do learn it.

Once you master this concept, it is far easier to indulge in a loving relationship with someone, knowing the big picture. When a confrontation with someone begins, just ask yourself: "What is this person trying to teach me here and how can I respond to him/her without overreacting?" This is not an easy lesson to learn.

You will forget, get mad, start the big drama, and escalate it into a big disaster. Okay, then, you made a mistake. If you are not able to meet that person again at a later time to say you are sorry or to speak whatever is on your mind—your truth—then you just need to visualize that person in your mind. Ask for forgiveness for yourself, or maybe you need to forgive the individual because you didn't do anything wrong. Just forgive and let it go.

If you still find it hard to forgive, ask God to help you discover a new direction within your heart. Do not let your mind wander into self-destructive talk about why you said this, or did that, or what you should have said.

If that kind of mind chatter begins, just notice it and refuse to unconsciously drift into that negative thinking. Move your thinking and attitude back to love of self, forgiveness, and being grateful for the lesson that person taught you.

This kind of positive thinking will serve you well in your lifetime. It will help you to keep your relationships moving in the right direction of self-growth, love, and nurturing. Remember that they are all just lessons.

There is no wrong way. There is no judgment if you make the incorrect action the first time around. God does not judge you. God is not disappointed in you. God only loves you and wants you to love yourself. The self-knowing power and wisdom about self-responsibility all resides within your own heart. Your heart knows what is ethical and what is the right action; it knows your truth, and it knows the lessons you need to learn. Just observe what happens in your life and watch it unfold.

Learn to listen to your own inner voice. It only speaks truth. You have this inner wisdom. Learn to listen to it and trust it.

I have introduced many concepts here: Self-love, self-responsibility, truth, ethics, compassion, karma, judgment, forgiveness, inner-wisdom, and trust. These are simple words but huge in meaning. You might not learn these moral principles all at once or they may not come easily. It may take as long as a lifetime or several lifetimes to understand and master these concepts.

All I would like to instill in you is the notion of trusting your inner voice and an understanding of the Universal Laws and Principles. Trust your heart and be confident you are exactly where you are supposed to be every minute of your life. Everything is as you planned it. This is truly the power that resides within you. God is there to support you and love you. But you need to do the work.

You really do have the power to control your own life by the choices you make. You take responsibility for your actions and your thoughts—no one else. You are never alone in this. God, your higher self, your other guides, and teachers are always there to help you along. They guide you through your life to be at the right place at the right time so you can fulfill your contract in this lifetime.

You may ask, "Why does it have to be this way?" It is because you are a god in training. Remember that you chose this physical body in this lifetime to learn certain lessons. You are really a spirit in a physical body (your latest car) coming to this earth classroom to learn your lessons.

Think of yourself as an angel being born on earth in a physical body so you can experience life through your five senses, and all your myriad of emotions. We all must come to this physical plane in order to experience these things. We cannot experience them at the higher planes of existence.

In the spirit world, things move at a slower pace. In the physical world, our growth moves much faster because of our senses and emotions. It is the reason so many souls are all clamoring to come to Planet Earth right now to experience the density of a physical body. We advance more quickly as souls in the physical realm. We have been given an incredible opportunity as gods-in-training to experience this physical plane.

You may not think so when you are having a disagreement with someone or when you are trying to learn a new skill and you feel stupid because you can't do it properly. Just step back, take a deep breath, and know everything is in right order. Nothing is wrong. It is only a lesson and sometimes we have to practice for a while.

It is really an adventure in learning about the power of you!

CHAPTER 7

The Power of Meditation

To make the right choices in life, you have to get in touch with your soul. To do this, you need to experience solitude, which most people are afraid of because in the silence you hear the truth and know the solutions.

– DEEPAK CHOPRA

Listen to your own inner voice to access the Power of Me!

In this chapter you will learn the power of using meditation, with some simple tips to help you manifest whatever you want.

The powerful practice of meditation opens up your conscious mind to the wonders of your inner world. All you need to do is sit in a relaxed position with your eyes closed and melt into your inner peace. It sounds effortless yet, for most of my life, I was not the best student.

Over the years I have been gently nudged and encouraged to stop and listen to this inner voice. Sometimes that nudge would be a notation in a book, another's suggestion or whispers in my own head to sit down, breath, relax, and listen, or to simply write my response. I heard the message repeatedly in many formats to stop my "busyness," become quiet and relaxed, and tune in. Sometimes I listened; most of the time I ignored it.

Fortunately, that inner voice is really persistent and quite loud, so it can rise above my inner chatter and mental clutter. I have read many books, attended classes, and participated in many groups on meditation and none of it has come easily or sunk in about how to achieve it gracefully. For some reason, I have always resisted being quiet, and it seems to be a common dilemma for most of us.

Other resources suggest you should quiet the mind by removing all thoughts and take deep breaths. Well, for me, that lasts about five seconds and my mind starts chattering again. How can I hear God, my higher self, guides or teachers with this racket?

Some people suggest repeating a mantra (a chanting of words or a phrase) over and over again, which helps one get into a place of "emptiness." Writing always seemed to work the best for me.

As I have grown older and maybe a bit wiser, I look back at my life or reread some of my writings and understand now that I have been meditating—or, rather, listening—to my inner voice all along. It is just a very subtle, quiet voice that suggests loving thoughts and then waits to see how I respond. I have learned to trust this wise voice.

At some point one needs to learn how to differentiate one's personality/ego voice from the inner spiritual voice. I had to learn to look and listen with my "God eyes and ears" and lots of practice.

To reach a quiet place of relaxation, breathing, and listening, I needed to find a way to get into that zone of stillness, inner-awareness, and receptivity. Many times I would make up my own meditations or prayers; other times I would participate in a guided meditation, in which I listened to someone else lead me through a setting, such as down a path or hallway or up a mountain trail.

Searching for the many ways to relax my mind and discover my inner awareness and silence became my initial intent. Once arriving in this beautiful quiet place, I was now ready to openly accept the information or experience a blissful moment.

Simply listening to soft instrumental music also helps me to relax and quiet my mind, as opposed to loud Heavy Metal music or vocals. I have experienced many beautiful visions by simply listening to the music and letting my mind wander out into the ethers.

In the early stages of developing my abilities, I discovered that the best technique for me was to sit in a quiet, relaxing place such as in my bed early in the morning, with a pen and paper. I would close my eyes, ask a question, and wait for an answer.

A few hints I learned along the way: First, it is important to allow the words to flow without interruption. Write the first thing that comes into your mind until you feel complete with it. Don't worry about misspelling or questioning whether you have found the right word. Keep going.

Second, do not stop, reread, analyze or edit while the words are flowing through you. You will lose your train of thought and the meaning you want to convey. You can do that only after you have completely finished writing your thoughts. Remember that the answer you receive may not make sense to you at that time anyway. Keep your analytical mind out of it.

Frequently, I have gone back several weeks later and reviewed some of my writing and was astonished at the wisdom of my message. It didn't make sense at the time of the writing but, as I looked back at my life, what I wrote had actually happened, or I gained some profound clarity on some issue that was troubling me. I was so amazed.

If writing doesn't come easily for you, just take your time with it and practice or search for something you enjoy doing. Don't force yourself to do something you hate.

I also sit at a computer and write out my answers because I am a fast typist. It works great for me, but only take that approach if it feels right for you.

Instead of writing, you could also talk into digital recorder or Dragon software. Record all your thoughts, feelings, sensations, symbols, and whatever comes to you—again, no editing. Just let the words flow.

Another technique for getting into the quiet zone is to start by simply thinking of something pleasant like nature. Let's do this together.

- Sit in a comfortable chair, with your feet flat on the floor and hands placed gently on your lap.
- Take a few deep breaths, close your eyes, and just feel yourself relax.
- Continue with slow deep breaths noticing each in-breath and out-breath, as well as the pause in between.
- Next, gently move your mind into a meadow, for example, with a babbling brook and sit down in the cool grass and admire the beauty of where you are.
- Ask a question or simply feel the relaxation of being in such a beautiful place. Continue to focus on your breath. Request that one of your guides appear to you and then ask him or her a question. Or you may simply relax deep into your body and mind enjoying the beautiful surroundings.

It is amazing what will appear before you. Enjoy the moment. By now you may have gone so far into this peaceful, relaxed place that you have forgotten about your body. It is almost as if you can't even feel it.

When you linger in a beautiful place of complete relaxation for a while and transcend your physical body, you begin to experience the most amazing sensations. You feel like you are separate from your body, floating somewhere out in the ethers. Do not be concerned or think something is wrong. Enjoy the peaceful moment. You have found your "blissful" place within your spiritual heart. Feel and cherish this moment.

If meditation is so blissful, why have I resisted the experience all these years? For me, being in a deep state of relaxation felt extraordinary, yet it was very difficult for me to come out of it. At times I did not want to return to my physical body and ego/personality again. Sometimes fear engulfed me. I was afraid I couldn't solidly return and ground myself back into my body or that maybe I would lose my mind; all fears that I had to overcome.

These represent my issues; you may have others. The important thing is to become aware of your blocks and keep practicing until you move through it.

My excuses were numerous for why I couldn't possibly stop, relax, breathe, and meditate. I resisted for years. My role as a mom, corporate executive, wife, daughter, sister, and many others, kept me so busy that I was too exhausted to find a moment to relax. I just couldn't turn off the brain and slow down. If I sat down to relax, I would just fall asleep.

However, as I have grown older, with a physical body that insists I slow down, I am learning to enjoy those quiet moments. I am listening to my inner voice more easily. In fact, I have written this whole book listening to my inner voice. Once I surrendered to this process, I felt my resistance and fears melt away. I recently learned that resistance is part of the meditative process especially for beginners. I now visualize my resistance as a challenging stumbling block I must rise above in order to move from my conscious/ego mind into my unconscious meditative state. With this understanding, I now resist less and wait for me to jump over the hurdle to my place of bliss. I accept the challenge and continue to practice.

If fitting time to meditate each day is an issue, here's one easy place to begin:

Sit quietly and comfortably for five minutes each day and focus on your thoughts, feelings, and bodily sensations. Relax and let go of everything. Your intent is to tune into yourself and be present. As you do this each day, you will get used to listening to yourself and hearing your inner voice—a good place for a beginner to start learning the process. Challenge yourself to fit five minutes into your day to spend time with yourself.

As noted earlier, mastering the art of meditation can be difficult for many people. Life pulls us into many directions, focusing primarily on our physical bodies, relationships, and our outer world.

Many styles of meditation are available to you. Some will facilitate your process; others will not. I encourage you to explore the different types of meditation to find your world of inner awareness and your present moment of *now*. Do some research and choose whatever methods work best for you. There are several techniques that can point the mind in the right direction. Search for an instructor, read books, attend classes or research online for what appeals to you.

Mediation is an important skill to master, as this is where you will develop a relationship with God. Since most of us carry the lesson in this life to find our way back home to God, meditation offers one way to achieve this. I hope your path of meditation is easier than mine.

Listen for your inner voice deep inside yourself, always there, waiting for you. Enjoy your peaceful journey by entering your heart's inner sanctuary.

CHAPTER 8

The Power of Manifestation

Believing in and living by faith on the Living One inside of you, activates a mighty spiritual magnet that draws the Miraculous to you.

– VIDWAN

Imagine the power to shape your life the way you want!

If you ask yourself, "Wow, can I really do that?" you will hear a resounding, "YES, YOU CAN!"

As a co-creator, you truly hold the power within you to shape your world. The art of manifestation unfolds as your *intent in action*—a truly powerful gift. Learn to have fun with it. Play with it and observe your daily interactions as they change shape, shift, and change. You are that powerful!

The definition of *manifestation*, according to the dictionary, doesn't really express the meaning I am referring to here. One dictionary refers to it as "readily perceived by the senses, especially the sight." Another definition is to "display or demonstrate." A more accurate description that I like is based on the word *manifesto*, which means a "public declaration of intentions, motives or views."

To put manifestation into practice, you would have a thought or desire, create and express your intention, and the result would be a display or demonstration of your thought acting it out or producing the desired result. One could also call this the "art of positive thinking," and represents the practicality of spirituality. You bring your thought from the spiritual realms and ground it into a physical manifestation producing an outcome.

To practice this skill, start with small practical things. For example, I like to manifest parking places. It usually works about ninety percent of the time.

Imagine driving around in your car looking for a parking place in a huge, busy parking lot. One hint is that if you know the parking lot will be busy ahead of time, begin your thought or visualization to find the perfect parking place even before you arrive. I begin by calling out to my "parking angels" (which is my higher self or whoever will listen) and ask for the perfect spot to become available right now.

I usually head for the first few rows close to the store I want to visit—definitely positive thinking on my part. I drive up and down the rows still visualizing my parking place and, sure enough, someone will be pulling out of a space just as I approach.

I then pull into my manifested parking place, all excited and giggling that once again, I succeeded. I thank my "parking angels" for their assistance and feel appreciation and gratitude for another display of my power to manifest. Leaving their parking places presented perfect timing for those individuals and perfect timing for me—all in alignment and in right order.

This is often called the Law of Attraction. It means that when you focus your thoughts and energy on something specific, you will receive the outcome you want.

You can do this with anything. The desire and feeling must come from your heart and can only be intended for the highest good of yourself and others. You can never do it to harm someone or to create a "spell." If you attempted to cast a spell, you would harm the other person as well as yourself. In addition, you would create a karmic situation in which, somewhere down the line, someone will do the same evil deed to you. Furthermore, you would not be in a place of integrity, honesty, and self-responsibility.

You can start with small things like parking places and continue all the way up to joining and influencing the collective thought forms of the world *for the good of all.*

For example, many people have a planetary thought form (conscious or unconscious) that it is acceptable to damage the earth by polluting and destroying its resources, without any consideration for the planet or making any effort to replenish those resources. You have the power to change that harmful collective thought. It first starts with you.

- A good technique for beginning any manifestation or meditation is to begin by sitting quietly with your feet flat on the floor.
- Breathe deeply, close your eyes, relax, and ground yourself by feeling yourself sitting purposefully in your chair.
- Focus on your breath to facilitate relaxation. One suggestion is to place your attention on one of your higher-self points such as your third eye between and slightly above your eyebrows. Now think of the Mother Earth and see and feel the pollution or whatever the problem is. Ask your angels for assistance in amplifying the vibrations of your desire by sending love and white light to those around you or to the whole planet. Use your imagination to express your intent and thoughts wrapped in the power of love, harmony, joy, and balance, in whatever way works for you.
- Now shift that thought to where you see a clean, beautiful, balanced Mother Earth, free of pollution and where all of humanity has learned how to use the earth's resources in a loving way instead of a destructive way, and, most importantly, adding in the powerful emotion of appreciation for the gifts the earth provides for us. Visualize your desired manifested thought and then you move that thought to your heart, where you add your intense emotion and feelings such as love and appreciation. Hold that manifested thought for as long as you feel it is appropriate and when you feel complete with it.

- Next, work to find ways you will not pollute your environment. You will not throw that plastic cup on the ground or even throw it in the trash. You will find a way to recycle it. By changing your personal behavior and thought patterns, plus manifesting a new world vision of living in peace and harmony with Mother Earth, you will assist in changing the collective mind. If you do this in a group, this thought form expands exponentially.

We really are that powerful. The above outcome will take a bit longer than manifesting a parking space, but it will be achieved if we all focus our minds on a "clean" planet. Mother Earth is ready and waiting, and I believe the younger generation with the "new" children coming forward will make it happen.

So, start manifesting those little things and work up to the grand ideas and see what you can accomplish. Remember that as you change, grow, and learn the Power of Me, the whole planet changes, because collectively, we are an all powerful *one*.

A few more hints: Practice the art of manifesting what you want in your life by asking your higher self, guides, spiritual teachers, and God for what you want using precise and specific wording. If you want something to happen now, say so. The trick is to ask, set your exact intention, and then wait for the universe to act.

If you don't ask, the universe won't do it for you. I would like to emphasize how important it is to earnestly request what you want in your life, from simple things like finding your car keys to larger issues such as a relationship. Some requests produce results immediately while others take longer to manifest. After you have completed the step of asking for what you want, shift your words and thought patterns to "*I have*" this desired result. Visualize it happening. Another very powerful manifesting phrase is "*I am*." For example, whatever words you place after "I am," you become it, such as "I am prosperous;" "I am healthy;" "I am confident;" "I am love;" and "I am one with God." Make your own list and incorporate these affirmations into your life to create your desired reality.

Keep an open mind, with no expectations and be patient. What we think we need, may not be what God and our soul think we need. Again, trust that everything is progressing, as it should according to your mission.

So be precise in your intent and keep asking with an open heart. But be careful what you wish for. You will be surprised by what you can manifest. Practice this great skill and honor this gift. It will serve you well as you go through your life, co-creating with God.

CHAPTER 9

Your Personality/Ego versus Your Higher Mind

*All that we are is the result of what we have thought.
What we think, we become.*

– Buddha

Our ultimate goal in this current timeframe on earth is to open up and re-awaken our higher mind by understanding and rising above the enticements of our everyday ego/personality. Our higher mind is always connected to our God Source, yet the ego seems to dominate as we become distracted by the physical attractions of life.

You may think your ego and higher mind are acting as one, but there is a distinction between the two. Your ego represents your personality in this lifetime only, expressed as the "I," meaning "I want something for me in this everyday world."

The ego acts like a mediator between self and your outer reality and is not part of your soul memories. Many refer to it as the lower mind where we experience duality and where ego takes over our mental mind. Ego rules, analyzes, defends, rationalizes, procrastinates, and controls the personality. The ego/personality is also what you perceive as a separation between you and your god-self.

Love transforms the illusion of separation into a higher state of oneness. The purpose of the "higher mind" of consciousness is to EXPERIENCE and represents the "we," or the collective consciousness, of where we recognize the *"other."*

This higher mind is part of your soul-self, connected to your God source, and accompanies you for every lifetime. When you are in your higher mind, you are so aware of the "other" that you are driven to be of service to others. Your higher mind also brings you to a place of unconditional love for self and for others.

In this lifetime, we spend most of our time pivoting between these two minds, so it will prove helpful for you to understand the difference between "me" and the "other."

As a baby you are so aware of your physical body that you spend your days exploring it and your external world. You love to experience everything and everyone, soaking up the new sensations of every moment of your day. As an infant, your ego and personality begin to develop and, basically, at this point, your ego governs and guides this part of your mind as you explore the world with your five senses.

The personality/ego perceives only through your five senses and feels several emotions, including negative ones such as fear, anger, impatience, etc. The ego becomes your guide and acts as a protector in this physical world, encompassing a great purpose and functioning initially so you can experience all your emotions and physicality.

It functions constantly to analyze, rationalize, and judge everything and everybody. As you grow older, you generally still focus on the "me."

For example, you focus on your physical appearance, your clothes, your hair, and what others think of you. You also decide to play a particular role in life. What will you grow up to be? You start to think about your career choices, college, marriage, etc.

We make judgments. We measure everything by certain standards that we learned from our relationships and our environment over time. If these judgments and measurements become too entrenched, we get stuck in ego (personality) and struggle to move into our higher mind or even forget that we have a higher mind.

Many times fear holds us back from moving from the ego mind to the higher mind. Eventually, as we mature, most of us wake up to our true soul-self and move to our higher mind and are aware of it.

Opening up and becoming awake and consciously aware of your soul-self is crucial, whereby you shift from the "me" to the "other" by demonstrating care, compassion, and unconditional love for the other without expectations.

The ego feeds on feelings of self-importance and grandeur.

When you can move beyond these feelings of self-importance and move more toward caring for others, you move closer to living in unconditional love within your higher mind. When you move into your higher mind, you link to the universal mind of God.

Learning the difference between your ego mind/personality and your higher mind is another big test.

Ask yourself, "Can I recognize myself as the higher mind and transmute (change), transform (bring the experience to light), transcend (rise above negative thought), move out of my ego personality, and find my higher mind?"[17]

We have the power to make the shift. Become aware of the difference between the lower ego mind and your higher mind. The ego lower mind is the chatterbox in your head. Tell your controlling ego mind loudly to be still if it still chatters on.

For example, talk to your ego/personality like a friend and say the following:

Ego, you have my permission to stop controlling my thoughts. I can manage them on my own now. I make the choices of what I will think, whether positive or negative, and I am consciously aware of my thoughts. Ego, you can go back to playing the protector role, and I thank you for this important lesson. You taught me to maneuver my way from my ego/personality in this lifetime to my higher soul mind—my true self, the empowered co-creator that I am.

Try this dialogue with yourself. I found it to be a good technique to bring my mind back to conscious, positive thought, instead of being on automatic pilot.

Love of self and self-importance are distinctly different in connotation. Self-importance projects the feeling that you are better than someone else. Within this feeling exists a hierarchy of many judgments, fears, and separations.

Loving yourself forms a bridge between yourself and others, ideally sharing the emotion of love in a give-and-receive interaction without expectations, conditions or judgments. Wait to hear that soft voice within. Begin to learn to listen for your soul to guide you. This is your true voice.

Bring the experience to the light of your awareness, and rise above the negative thinking. Focus your attention on your thoughts through the process of self-observation. A strong will is what is required to focus your attention and hold it there. Begin to change; it is a goal worth striving for. Again, it is part of your test, so study hard. Be conscious of your thoughts. Are they positive or negative? Listen to yourself. Activate the power within you to be awake and aware of where your mind travels.

Make the leap forward to live life consciously free of roadblocks such as fear and other dramas, fervently knowing your thoughts have wings to shape-shift your inner and outer world. When you become aware of your inner relationship with self, no matter what is reflected in your outer world, eventually your outer world begins to mirror your inner world of peace. That is your power.

The vibrant light within your higher mind waits for you to discover how to overcome roadblocks such as fear, and transmute your negative emotions into the opposite virtues of courage, confidence and love.

CHAPTER 10

The Big and Little Fears and Oh, Yes, the Fear of Death

Remembering that you are going to die is the best way I know to avoid the trap of thinking you have something to lose. You are already naked. There is no reason not to follow your heart.

Stay hungry. Stay foolish.

– Steve Jobs, CEO of Apple, Inc., Commencement address delivered at Stanford University in 2005

Overcoming and understanding our fears is probably the hardest lesson we will learn in our lifetime. In order to conquer them, it helps to dissect our imaginary and very real fears, so we can see how irrational they often appear.

Webster's Dictionary defines fear as "an unpleasant, often strong emotion caused by expectation or awareness of danger." Another definition of fear is "False Evidence Appearing Real."[18] Perhaps it could also be defined as "some perceived, imaginary illusion appearing real."

When I think about my fears, I find it very difficult to wrap my head around the concept of them as "false evidence" or illusions. They sure feel real to me, both physically and emotionally.

Our physical brain interprets our environment as matter, but we also have a part within our brain, known as the limbic system, specifically the amygdala, that processes the sensory input of emotion, such as fear.

At times, the emotional part of our brain perceives information from our environment as fearful.

In other words, we perceive something in our surroundings as a danger and respond to this physical environment with an emotional response of fear.

A very vivid example of an imaginary fear happened to me around the age of seven or eight. I remember waking up in the middle of the night and seeing what looked like eerie eyes looking at me from across my bedroom. It felt so scary to me at the time. I would hide my head under the covers hoping it would go away. I would occasionally peek out from the covers and still see those eyes. Eventually, I did go back to sleep.

The next morning, when I awoke to a bright sunny day, I recalled the memory of those fearful eyes and looked over at the dresser area where they had watched me the night before. There I saw my camera with a flash attachment on it that, in reality, was just a light reflection, not a menacing pair of peering eyes. I gave out a hearty laugh at myself and sighed with relief.

This offered quite a lesson in distinguishing between the flicker of light and darkness and how fear played a role in teaching me about this illusion—a vivid demonstration of "false evidence appearing real." My imagination had created this whole story in my mind and I interpreted it as real. This represented one of those times when my rational brain explained away the fear.

Oftentimes the emotion of fear and its source can be difficult and disturbing to sort through since it does not always reveal itself in a clear, conscious, and understandable pattern. Many of our old unconscious memories from our past can be spontaneously expressed later in life without understanding their source. Major fears haunt our lives, such as fear of failure, of not fitting in and ending up alone, of abandonment, of danger or getting hurt, and many more—including the fear of death, the biggest fear of all for most people.

If a fear lingers for a long period of time, it could eventually start manifesting into physical symptoms. Therefore, understanding the relationship between our brain, our emotions, and our behavior, offers us a vital key to avoiding illness. You will find volumes written about fear and how it affects our behavior and how to overcome it.

Most importantly, realize that fear holds you back from experiencing your important lessons in this lifetime. Embrace risk and change in your life beyond fear and without holding back. Imagine how your life could blossom if you had no fear. Leap ahead with courage and enthusiasm, commanding your fears to step aside.

I emphasize that overcoming our fears is one of the main lessons of this lifetime. We must learn to walk through our fears without holding life at arm's length. Confront your fears. Try to understand their complexities, moving toward forgiveness, love, and surrender. This will take a lifetime or two; so don't think that you will figure it all out in the next week or so.

Part of our life's contract is to put situations onto our path so we will experience and feel the fear, then see how we will respond or behave. Some of those responses will include you screaming and running the other way as fast as you can because you sense some danger or have some preconceived expectation of a specific outcome.

You may become angry or defensive in reaction to your fears. Whatever your response, you will be presented with the problem repeatedly until you can face the fear, see it, feel it, love it, and respond in a way that is not fearful or hurtful to yourself or others any longer. The people, places or problems will change, but the same lesson will be presented to you until you master it.

Don't get discouraged; patience and persistence are necessary for a successful outcome. Frequently, our most difficult challenges produce the greatest rewards. This is part of the duality—the positive and the negative—that we are learning on Planet Earth. It goes with the territory as part of the experience.

I once asked my higher self why I chose to come to earth and live in all this fear and negativity, since I don't like it much. The response was "to learn from experience within the physical realm." Well, okay then, but some of these fearful experiences are not a lot of fun. I realized I must learn to understand my fears and just face them. So I will keep practicing and working on it.

Another example that I am practicing to overcome is a fear of public speaking. In order to overcome it, when I worked in a corporate job, I would intentionally put myself into situations where I would have to speak before groups of people. I forced myself to practice public speaking, which helped me overcome my fear. It is not easy. Sometimes I could walk right up to that podium and just do it with no problems. Every now and then my voice would crack and I could feel that fear creeping in again.

Another situation occurred when I became a teacher in an adult education class. At first I spoke nervously before the whole class, but soon I began talking as though simply addressing one person. It became easier and easier the more I did it.

This is an example of facing your fears, considering that the fear of speaking is not as huge as, perhaps, a fear of dying or fear of abandonment or other such experiences in which one does not really have a lot of control over the situation. Just remain aware of your fears and work on them in your own way and in your own time.

We all eventually eliminate most of our fears and fulfill the truth of who we are— spiritual beings having physical experiences.

So, if you have a fear of talking in public, just go to that next party, that next interview or that next board meeting and walk into that room and start looking into the eyes of your audience; talk to people from your heart. Just love them. Don't hold back from the love you could receive by being the true person you are; don't hold life at arm's length. Embrace everyone.

At times this may be hard to do… such as when your friend or co-worker gets in your face, for example, and gossips about someone. Simply listen, but make an agreement with yourself not to participate or to judge anyone. Just try it. Take a breath, and take a moment, then go back and remind yourself again about the principle discussed earlier to take personal responsibility for your actions.

You are only responsible for you. Don't give in or succumb to fear by joining in the gossip just so you can feel like you belong. Make the choice not to gossip. Take the risk, walk through your fear of feeling left out, stand your ground, be true to yourself and demonstrate kindness. In the end, you will have the respect of your friends because they will know you are not a gossip. You can be trusted with their secrets. And you will have successfully overcome your fear of not fitting into the group by not joining in on the gossip.

Fear can be so scary that it can make you want to hide under the covers and just stay in bed all day! I hope you will give yourself a pat on the back for facing your fears, taking responsibility for your actions, and being true to yourself!

We also need to understand that fear results from believing we are separate from God. It is a feeling of disconnectedness, aloneness, separation, or loss. This separation causes a deep anxiety. It starts as a thought in our mental body that says, "Oh, I am not good enough," which then moves into the emotional body as we begin to feel the anxiety and fear. This emotion eventually manifests itself in DIS-EASE, or illness in the physical body. Sometimes these fears stay with us from lifetime to lifetime, especially if there has been some kind of trauma.

I'd like to share with you another simple example from my childhood. I used to think a boogieman or a ghost lurked under my bed. Whenever I would wake up in the middle of the night, I used to dread getting out of bed and putting my feet down on the floor. I thought for sure someone was going to grab my feet.

I am not sure what "they" would do with me once they caught me but, rational or not, my fear was very real. Maybe they would take me to some dark hole. My imagination conjured up all kinds of scary scenarios. It started as a frightening thought in my imagination, and then I experienced the emotion of fear. I felt the tension and anxiety in my physical body. As I grew older, I overcame the fear but even as an adult, once in a while, I would go back to that thought.

Now, as an adult, I understand and trust my own inner strength and know nothing under my bed will hurt me. Maybe there really was a ghost there; I have seen them as well. So, if it is other beings, entities, angels, ghosts, demons, or whatever label you want to give it, I will just tell them, (in my mind, or talk out loud) to simply leave. I know now that I have that kind of inner power.

If an entity or something creates fear in you, trust that it is not right for you. You do have the power to ask it to leave. Say: *In the name of love and light, I (your name) request you to leave from under my bed. You are creating fear in me and I don't wish to feel that from you. I give back to you your fear. I wrap you and myself in love and white light.* Visualize yourself sending love to the entity and also wrapping yourself in love and white light. (We will look at some more examples of this in the next chapter.)

Many of our fears originate from our current lifetime only. However, some can stem from what is termed a "bleed through" or memory from a previous lifetime. Current lifetime fears often reflect our old internal fears. They have their roots in childhood traumas caused by a playmate, a parent, a sibling, an animal or a stranger—anyone.

Fear can also serve as a protective mechanism from danger. If a dangerous situation presents itself, fear sets in so we can respond quickly to it. In this instance, fear assists us to find safety. However, some fears can hold us back even to the point of withdrawing from life.

The most positive approach to eliminating fear is to expose yourself to it, if possible, in a safe, controlled manner, such as the way I conquered my fear of public speaking. I just did it over and over until I could walk past my fear.

Love all your fears. If one sets in, take a breath and send love to that fear. It has a calming effect so you can rationally look at the fear and find a way to deal with it. Seek additional help if necessary. Face your fears, love your fears, and take the risk to overcome them.

Remember that you are never alone in this journey. When you are no longer afraid, you will look at life more calmly without that nagging gut feeling of anxiety. Explore life free from fear and the door of opportunity will fly open for you. Fly free like an eagle to the top of the mountain, without the fear of flight weighing you down, and observe the metamorphosis of your eagle wings becoming angel wings.

Fear of Death

Fear of death presents a very hard lesson for all of us, no matter what our age. Young people are usually not exposed to death at an early age, but some children do have to face it, whether it occurs to a loved one or even a pet. Therefore, it is important to have an understanding from a broader perspective.

My daughter Erin's first impression of death occurred when she was five years old, while watching the movie called "Charlotte's Web." When Charlotte, the spider, died, my daughter became so upset and began sobbing so hard, that I had to put her to bed. No amount of hugs, kisses, and simple explanations of death would console her young innocent mind.

As she grew older, she eventually recovered and understood the process. Becoming older does not make it any easier to handle the loss of a loved one; it is just easier to understand. Five is very young age to understand such a huge concept of being human where one minute you are here in the physical body and the next minute you are gone.

To help you understand this more fully and to look at it from a more expansive spiritual viewpoint, I will share another story with you about my father's pet duck, Daffy.

One day I was reminiscing about Dad and Daffy and remembered the great relationship those two shared. I recalled how that duck loved my dad and would follow him all around the yard as he did his yard work. Daffy would eat worms, grass, and leaves as my dad dug up the dirt. It was always such an endearing scene to watch those two interact with each other. He was such a delight and brought our family so much joy.

Daffy loved the yard and never wandered away. Dad kept him in a pen in the garage during the cold Minnesota winters because he would never survive on his own. He was completely reliant on us for his feeding and care. In the spring, when we could let Daffy out of his winter cage, he was so excited to be out in the sunlight again, eating fresh goodies from the ground.

One year when the duck was about five years old, Daffy and my dad were digging and foraging as usual out in the crisp fall air. At one point, Daffy must have wandered off on his own to another part of the yard. Out of the corner of my dad's eye, he saw a big hawk come down and swoop up Daffy and carry him away. It was so sudden.

My dad was devastated, as we all were, when we heard the news. We all felt sad and mourned the loss of our dear friend. But I also felt my dad's heartache because he shared the closest relationship with Daffy. We knew he was hurting.

This death was a hard lesson for him to accept. We watched him and ourselves go through the normal stages of handling the grief when someone dies. We asked ourselves how one could cope with a death.

At first my dad felt total shock, emotional pain, and guilt. If only he could have been closer to Daffy and prevented the hawk from swooping him away. His second reaction was to become upset and sad at the loss, then mad at the hawk for stealing his pet. He asked, "Why did this happen? Why did God take away the friend I loved?"

It is normal to experience all of these emotions. Please allow yourself to express the multitude of feelings by crying or whatever you need to do to release the pain, sadness or other emotions. Grief is really your expression of the love you have for a person or creature. It may seem irrational and out of control to endure all of these feelings, but it is important to let yourself experience these stages of grief.

However, when you have deeply cried your eyes out enough, stand back and reflect on what happened from a cosmic perspective. This will help you accept and understand the purpose of death. In the end, you may eventually arrive at a place where you will not fear death.

Daffy chose to live his life in captivity with our family rather than in the wild. It is what he wanted to experience in that lifetime. He CHOSE to die at the hands of the hawk. It was his time to die and transition out of his current body and move to another realm for a while, or maybe even be born again to another lifetime on earth, often referred to as reincarnation.

Daffy also knew he would be providing food for the hawk, who must also live out its lifetime. And that was a good thing for the hawk. It was a shared agreement at the soul level that they each made to each other before they were born into physical bodies, so they could help each other.

As I look back on this experience in my life, I remember the trauma and sadness of his death, but I can now understand what it was all about. I think of Daffy and send him my love and thank him for giving me the chance to experience his life and love. I still miss watching him and my dad play in the yard, but we share this wonderful memory of him and our love for him will never die. It will remain a part of my mind even after I die.

I remind myself that it is only my physical body that goes away, not my higher mind. My soul lives on. In fact, in the next life, I will have a new body (a new car), a new life, new experiences, new lessons, and new memories to add to my Akashic Record. Wow, what an adventure. I wonder what kind of car Daffy is driving right now… Maybe he chose to be a dog in his next lifetime on earth…? Maybe he is a god in another universe…?

Death is not something I fear anymore. I understand that we live many lifetimes. We have many different bodies. Think of it as getting a new car every once in a while. The old car wears out, so you get a new one. But you still bring along all experiences, life lessons, and memories with you. Your soul lives on.

On an emotional and sensory level, I miss Daffy. I can no longer see him in his cute, cuddly duck form. I can't hold him and smell his duck feathers, and I won't hear his quacking sound as he comes running to us when we call him. We miss all of that, but it gives me comfort to understand he is happy in his new life. I know I will see him again in another life and in another form.

Death is not something to fear or dread; it is really just a transition from one life to another. Grasping the concepts of life, death and rebirth as purposeful, are hard at first. The idea that Daffy gave his life so another could live is a part of nature that I still grapple with, especially when it is my loved one choosing to transition. But I now accept it. I do not wish to diminish the immensity of the heartache, distress and anguish one feels when someone dies. Even though you can step back and look at the spiritual purpose of death, there is still tremendous, gut wrenching pain and loss that must be processed and endured. Allow that process to unfold.

I know my current life is just one moment in universal time. My soul lives on and on, and I will see my loved ones again. While I am in this physical body right now, I appreciate the magic of this moment. I appreciate the magic of my breath. I don't fear death. I am free from the grip of fear.

Think about this concept and see if you can find a place within yourself where you can set yourself free—free from fear and the fear of death.

Keep in mind that all your fears halt you in your tracks because resisting and holding back limits your soul journey. There will be times when you sink into your fears, but allow yourself to rationally step back and examine the universal, spiritual perspective. Expand your imagination and consider multiple possibilities and perspectives about life and death, keeping negative thoughts in check.

Listen to your inner voice, the one that says, "Yes, you can make the leap off that diving board of life." Dive in and enjoy the thrill and excitement, free from fear that comes from expanding your mind and stepping out into your power and moving forward into something new and different.

CHAPTER 11

I See Spooks in My Bedroom

There is no such thing as death. Life is only a dream, and we're the imagination of ourselves.

– Bill Hicks

Oh my! I have opened and expanded my imagination and sensitivities to my world and now I see spooks in my room. Now what?

The gift of sixth-sense sight has been bestowed upon you. Good work! A "spook" in your room is a manifestation of a spiritual soul and can be defined as a "paranormal experience."*

Scientific thought examines the "normal" according to our five senses and physical laws. Paranormal thought investigates the other side of "normal" utilizing our sixth sense. Many of us perceive the unexplained paranormal. We know what we see, hear, and feel no matter what our rational mind envisions.

Therefore, ghosts, or "spooks" as I sometimes teasingly call them, must be included in our multileveled reality and need to be part of the conversation when discussing the spiritual realms of angels and spiritual guides.

As Planet Earth increases her vibratory rate, an increasing number of people, and especially the perceptive children, are becoming more and more sensitive to their surroundings on all levels. This means that not only are our physical senses becoming more acute, but our extrasensory senses are also beginning to soar off the charts.

Extrasensory means perceiving something beyond our five senses. We tap into our "sixth sense," meaning that we expand our abilities to see, hear, feel, and even taste things that may not exist in the physical realm.

If we can accept our continuous evolvement in becoming multidimensional beings, or beings living beyond the Third Dimension, we can accept our many so-called strange but natural abilities such as seeing air, auras, blue lights, gold lights, hearing other people's thoughts, or even seeing so-called ghosts. I encourage you to be open to the possibility that this is the way the universe works.

Not everyone on earth will agree or accept this notion. Each soul is at a different level of evolvement, so not all are ready to see beyond the five senses. We should strive to walk in our own footsteps without judgment or intolerance of another's path. We all unfold at our own pace, with no hierarchy or expectation of another's higher or lower abilities and evolvement.

If you have not experienced any of these sensations or visions yet, do not concern yourself. All will happen in perfect order for you, when the time is right. You continually stay safe, protected, and in control.

However, if you do see them, and it becomes clear according to your perception that you have encountered ghosts or souls that have died or transitioned and you see or hear them, know that your feelings and perceptions portray the truth from a broad multidimensional perspective. Ideally, we view these encounters fearlessly and with a sense of control. Again, we are that powerful.

If you feel uncomfortable with some entity, you can ask it to leave the room. Most are lovable beings visiting you for the moment, or perhaps it is someone who has just transitioned and is wandering around for a while, before moving into the light.

Maybe you can ask these souls what they are doing there in your bedroom, and suggest they move to the light. You can help guide them if you wish, or ask that they move out of your vicinity. Thank them for their visit and say goodbye or "see you later" since you may meet them again someday or perhaps in another lifetime. Just follow your imagination and let it guide you as to what to do and say.

The important thing is not to be afraid. That can be easier said than done, of course, when they startle you in the middle of the night, as they hover at the end of your bed. Remember that we are all gods in training, co-creators and children of the Light. All entities embody the Light, yet some may at times stray from their path and create mischief while trying to sort out their newly perceived, and sometimes difficult shift, into the non-material realm.

This can create possible difficulties for you if they react with anger and meanness by refusing to take responsibility for their actions. Or, perhaps they are working out their karma at the moment and sharing it with you. Trust that you will know if an entity is making you feel fearful or uncomfortable and that you can just ask it to leave.

However, some may insist on lingering around, refusing to leave since they want to interact with your energy field in some way and stay with you or the place where you live or work. When this happens, initiate the following techniques to protect yourself and, hopefully, encourage the entity to move on. Note that, whether you see them or not, you can still use these protection techniques.

Entity Clearing and Protection Techniques

Begin by using a crystal or any other rock that calls to you. If using a stone, you can "program" it by first washing the rock in saltwater to wash off any other previous thoughts or intentions. Then hold the stone, or whatever object you choose, in your hand, close your eyes, and say:

"In the name of love and light, I program this stone to be my protector and guardian angel. The white light protects me. I command you, entity, to leave my room now and not return. Move to the light now, as it will take you safely home. It is my will so mote this be."*

Know that your guides, teachers and guardian angels are always with you and that you are putting that intent and energy of protection into a physical object to be with you in the physical world. Grounding your intentions into an object helps to solidify the intent. You can do this with several rocks and put them around your room, your house, and your yard, knowing that they are all your protectors in love, light, and harmony.

With this intent of protection around you and your environment, your elevated energy level and vibratory rate will discourage unwelcomed entities. You may still see others, but monitor how they make you feel. Many are there to assist and guide you, so be open to the experience. If you don't like it, ask it to leave and repeat the above "entity clearing and protection technique."

If you have a child whose fear is bubbling up over some unwanted entity, take one of your child's Teddy bears, a doll, or even a blanket, or whatever objects you or the child feel comfortable with, and ask all of his/her guides, teachers and God to bless this object and request that it become your child's protector. To clear your child's Teddy bear or doll, etc., just hold the item in your hand, close your eyes, and say:

"In the name of love and light, I cleanse this object of any old energy or thought patterns at all levels, all directions, all dimensions, and all parallels. I re-program this _______ (object) to be my protector or my child's protector and guardian angel. The white light protects me, (or her/him.). It is my will, so mote this be."

In the Native American traditions, smudging with a sage, sweet grass or other herb bundles will also help to remove unwanted energies and purify the area or a person. You can purchase these bundles at many of the metaphysical stores. Begin by concentrating on your intent to cleanse and purify, while moving into a meditative and ceremonial frame of mind connecting to spirit. Light the tip of the sage or herb bundle with a match or lighter allowing the flame to burn for a few moments, then blow out the flame and fan the smoke with a feather or wave the smoldering bundle around the room or over the body to cleanse you, objects, environments and negative thoughts. I usually hold a plate or other container under the incense, as smoldering pieces of herbs will drop off, so be careful as you wave the bundle. It has a distinct smell of sweetness as it burns, similar to incense used in a church. The smoke of the smudge represents the breath of the Creator, and is a powerful tool in cleansing, purifying, harmonizing and empowering you and your environment.

There are many other ways to set up protections; this offers some examples. Explore other ways that you are drawn to and what works for you.

Besides setting up objects for protection, you can also safeguard your own being at all levels—your physical, emotional, mental, and spiritual bodies.

I never really thought of myself as being anything more than a physical body. It never occurred to me that I have a mental, emotional, and spiritual body each interrelated and needing my focused awareness on each part. Fortunately, I learned a very valuable tool to increase my awareness of each of these bodies, and to understand how to align them into a place of balance and harmony.

I share this valuable tool with you, so you can incorporate the "Grounding, Clearing, Protection and Balancing" techniques into your life, especially now during this time of the Great Awakening. It may be the only tool that brings you back to a place of sanity amidst the chaos that can happen all around you.

Therefore, incorporating these techniques into your life for each of your bodies is extremely important as you begin the awakening process. If you can do them every day, it would be best.

Sometimes we get busy or we forget and then we start to feel drained emotionally or physically or we just may feel out of sorts and not be sure why. That is a big hint that we are out of balance, and the body subtly reminds us to ground, clear, balance, and protect our essence. These techniques, as explained below, have been called the "Basics" as coined by Angela DeBry,[19*] a doctor of divinity, spiritual teacher, healer, and channel. These methods have also been written about in Alijandra's* *Color Healing* book referred to earlier.[20]

There are four techniques or tools: grounding, clearing, protecting, and balancing. Whenever I feel over-energized, low in energy, out of balance, in need of protection or as though I have been hit with some negative energy, I utilize these basic techniques. When I am not feeling well and can barely get my head off the pillow, I definitely practice them. I usually do all four exercises at once, but occasionally I will only do one of them, such as the grounding technique if I feel light-headed and unstable in my body. Utilize one or all of these techniques using your own intuition.

With the increased energies and shifts occurring during the Great Awakening, I can sometimes feel very disoriented mentally, emotionally or physically. There are many symptoms of this energy shift. Physical issues can emerge, such as strange illnesses or pains, yet doctors cannot provide a diagnosis.

Sometimes you may hear ringing or a series of tones in the ears. Fatigue presents a huge challenge. Emotionally, you can have many mood swings—again, for no apparent reason. Mentally, you could also feel like you are in a fog and forget the most basic things in life.

Overall, you sense that something is changing in your body and in your world, but you can't quite put your finger on what it is. Whatever you sense or whatever symptoms you experience, know that these exercises will help you get back on track. Know that change is good and, in the end, usually for the better. (Note: Always seek medical advice if not sure about your symptoms.)

So surrender to the process. Allow it to flow. However, when you can't get your head off the pillow, incorporate these into your life.

First, I will give the definitions as channeled by DeBry and Alijandra, followed by the actual *Ground, Clear, Protection and Balance* techniques

Definitions of Grounding, Clearing, Protecting and Balancing:

Step 1 – Grounding. "Ground represents the lowest part, bottom, or base of something. Many Eastern, Celtic, and American Indian philosophies believe that the physical body is the base of the soul. They also believe that when you bring the physical body into harmony, you are actively manifesting your soul purpose within the physical. Thus, ignoring the physical body can cause disturbance in all other aspects of your life. A house not built on a solid foundation or 'ground' will fall."

Step 2 – Clearing. "Clear suggests a freedom from cloudiness, haziness, muddiness etc., either literally or figuratively. Through Kirlian photography, it has been shown that the human body, plants, and animals have an energy field around their bodies. Many cultures believe that this energy can be transferred from one individual to another, consciously or unconsciously. The theory is that if people collect others' emotions, feelings, etc., their energy field acts like a sponge and they begin to mirror others' challenges."

Step 3 – Protecting. "Protection means to shield from injury, danger or loss—to guard or defend."

Step 4 – Balancing. "Balance represents a state of equilibrium or equipoise—equality in amount, weight, value or importance between two things or the parts of a thing. Many of the early spiritual and physical philosophies looked at the human being as a series of components that must be maintained in balance or disease—'dis-ease'—would occur. The focus of any healing modality is to support the parts of the human essence to stay in a state of fluid balance just like nature."[21]

Ground, Clear, Protect and Balance Techniques

To keep yourself grounded, cleared, protected, and balanced, you are encouraged to incorporate these techniques into your day or whenever your body starts to feel out of alignment. As you practice these tools, your body perception will become finely tuned to these sensations. Eventually, your body will be so attuned to this alignment that it will feel uncomfortable if you forget to take a moment and include these tools into your day.

These four techniques, as interpreted and paraphrased by the author and her experiences, are based on DeBry and Alijandra's channelings as footnoted:[22]

– Ground – Clear – Protect – Balance

1. Ground yourself – Visualize a large cord coming off of your base chakra (near the coccyx bone at the end of your spine on your buttocks) and going deep into the earth and wrapping around a rock, crystal or whatever appeals to you. Make the grounding cord whatever color or design you want. You can also envision cords coming out of your feet and going deep into the earth. This exercise grounds you firmly to the earth.

2. Clear - Visualize that you are washing away, from head to toe, all impurities and toxic energies and everything at the physical, mental, emotional, and spiritual levels. Visualize that you are wrapped in white light or rainbows as they cleanse it all away from you and move the toxic energies toward the earth.

3. Protect - When you want to protect yourself or your surroundings, say:

*In the name of love and light, I call forth the four Archangels, Michael, Gabriel, Ariel, and Uriel, to set the protection around the four corners of this room (or house, office, school, car, airplane, yourself or whatever). I invoke the White Brotherhood symbol** to wrap all in protection and in all directions. (If doing this for someone else, say at the end—in alignment with love, light, free will, and balance.)*

Another way to protect your physical, emotional, mental, and spiritual bodies and strengthen your boundaries is to visualize yourself being wrapped in white light, the rainbow rays, a lead shield or chrome ball (which acts like a mirror and bounces negative energies back to the sender).

Program this exercise with your higher self so that when you say, "**Activate shields**," your higher self will automatically and quickly activate your protections in the way you have them set up.

4. Balance - Balance each of your seven major chakras. Chakra is a Sanskrit word meaning "wheel" or "turning." These are part of the thirteen rays of creation. Here we work with only seven of the color rays. (See graphic for placement of each major chakra within the body.) Eventually, as we awaken

---

** The White Brotherhood symbol embodies a circle with a cross within the circle (depicted as a white Celtic cross with a magenta background that is pinkish-purple in color). The White Brotherhood symbol does not refer to the white race on earth but to an extraterrestrial galactic organization of angels.

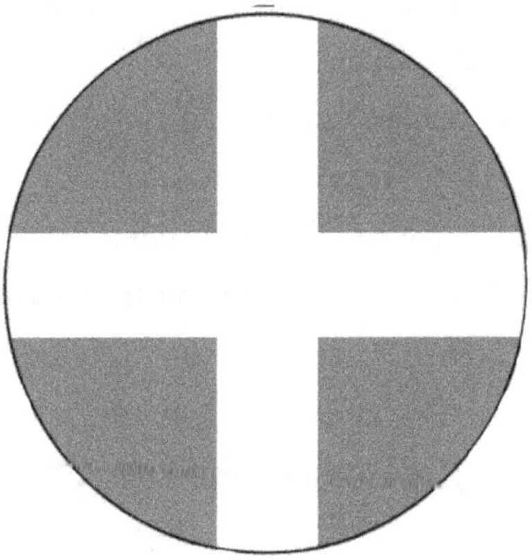

and move to a higher vibratory rate, we will open all thirteen of our chakras or the thirteen color rays of creation. Chakras are energy centers in the body expressing our life force. The primary seven centers are linked with our endocrine system, and align primarily along our spinal column. Each center connects our being at the physical, emotional, mental, and spiritual levels. Blocked energy can lead to physical illness or imbalances in our emotional and mental bodies. If you sense you are blocked or unbalanced, the following exercise will be restorative and revitalizing. The balancing exercise consists of starting at the base chakra and turning it three times to the right and then three times to the left. Move up to the next chakra and do the same for each until you get to the crown. Visualize each chakra as a spiral or a spinning wheel in the appropriate color ray of creation, as indicated in the detailed description below. Many times, each chakra will spin easily in both directions. Other days, you may be so out of balance; you perceive the spinning as difficult or even wobbly. Keep spinning until you feel more at ease and more aligned.

Chakra Exercise

- **Base (Root or Grounding) Chakra** – Located at base of the pelvis/coccyx bone. Visualize the spiral as the color red and spin it three times to the right and then three times to the left. Move up to the second chakra.

- **Second (Sexual or Creative) Chakra** – Located just below the belly button. Visualize the spiral as the color orange and spin it three times to the right and then three times to the left. Move up to the third chakra.
- **Third (Solar Plexus) Chakra** – Located just above the belly button. Visualize the spiral as the color yellow and spin it three times to the right and three times to the left. Move up to the fourth chakra.
- **Fourth (Heart) Chakra** – Located at your heart level between your breasts. Visualize the spiral as the colors emerald green for physical healing and pink for emotional healing. You can intertwine the pink and green into one spiral, or rotate each color separately, whatever you like. Spin the spiral(s) three times to the right and three times to the left. Move up to the fifth chakra.
- **Fifth (Throat)** Chakra – Located at your throat level. Visualize the spiral as the color of translucent blue or the color of the sky and spin it three times to the right and three times to the left. Move up to the sixth chakra.
- **Sixth (Third Eye)** Chakra – Located between the eyebrows and slightly higher. Visualize the color indigo (dark-purplish blue) and spin it three

times to the right and three times to the left. Move up to the seventh chakra.

- **Seventh (Spiritual) Crown Chakra** – Located at the top of the head and slightly toward the back of it. Visualize the spiral as the color violet and spin it three times to the right and three times to the left.

You have now reached a place of perfect balance. The first, second, and third chakras represent your physical body; the fourth and fifth chakras represents your emotional body; the sixth chakra or Third Eye* represents your mental body; and the crown chakra represents your spiritual body. When spinning the chakra to the right, you are balancing your male aspects; when spinning to the left, a balancing of your feminine aspects occurs.

The thirteen rays of creation, which include these seven, can also be incorporated into color healing using specific colors that represent a particular purpose. For example, the green ray at your heart chakra can facilitate the healing of either a section of or the whole physical body, depending on the focus of the ray's direction. Gently place your hands on your body or that of another person, and visualize the green ray facilitating the healing process as it permeates the area of intended focus.

Sometimes I will invoke the pink ray (representing unconditional love) to an area where I sense discord. The pink ray softens the energy creating a shift from the negative to the positive. I use this tool often. Simply visualize the color pink spreading through a room or surrounding an individual, and observe the subtle changes unfold. But, again, I refer you to Alijandra's *Healing with the Rainbow Rays, The Art of Color Energy Therapy,* as referenced in the bibliography, because the mastery of these concepts involves another book and area of study.

If you still feel fear, uneasiness, disempowered or a sense of being scattered (ungrounded), here is another simple tool to bring you back to the present moment so you can consciously focus on the Golden age unfolding before us. Call back all your energies, power and aspects of you that have either been taken from you or you willingly gave away to others creating disempowerment and unbalance. Visualize a large, warm sun slightly above your head. Now imagine you see a piece of you over there with your family, a particle of you with your job, a section of you in another lifetime, etc. Move all those aspects of you into the sun above your head filling it with all the scattered pieces of your being. Once you sense completion, slowly lower the sun downward over your body, wrapping you from head to toe. Then gently drop it into the earth for a complete grounding, cleansing, and balancing, as you restore yourself to your full angelic essence of empowerment.

In addition to these techniques, you may learn of others that feel right for you. Please use them if they are appropriate for you. Trust you are making the right choices for yourself. You have the power to make your own choices.

To reiterate, please do not become fearful of things you may not understand yet. I wish to share information about some of these possibilities because many people, especially the children, are seeing unexplained aberrations. I saw these things as a child; I see and feel them as an adult. I want you to be empowered and know what is going on rather than thinking you are wrong or going crazy or, worse yet, becoming fearful.

Many of the older adults show less sensitivity to these anomalies than the children do, since they were raised at a time on earth when the energy manifested at a much denser vibratory rate.

The children being born now (most, but not all) demonstrate more openness and more awareness of their conscious and unconscious minds, and their life in a multidimensional world. The new children know more than the older generations in many ways. These children will grow up and change the world to match their energies, so they, and Mother Earth, can all evolve into a more loving place. We honor these children for that lofty aspiration.

The older ones have been the stepping-stones. We began the process. It is now up to the children to fulfill God's future plan for our evolving planet.

These are some of the tools you will need throughout your awakening process. You will eventually learn when you are out of balance and not grounded. You will know when you have been hit by negative forces and need to clear it. By being "hit," I mean you could feel like someone just punched you in the stomach, or something as subtle as an unexplained, uncomfortable feeling in your body or in a physical location.

Just tune in to yourself and monitor how you feel. With practice, you will learn how to work with these transitioned souls or ghosts. Somehow, intuitively, I knew what to do.

For example, I have known two souls that have died and have assisted them in their transition to find what I perceived to be the tunnel of light. I was honored to help them. I have stood at the top of a temple at Chichen Itza in Mexico and felt the trapped souls be released as they walked up my body and out the top of the temple to the heavens. I have had many remarkable experiences such as these with transitioned souls. The gift they each gave me to remain unafraid of the paranormal and death is one I will always cherish.

As you go through your life, remember to always work in the name of love and light, and in alignment with love, light, free will, and balance.

CHAPTER 12

Dreams

Dreams are free, so free your dreams.

– Astrid Alauda

Dreams serve as the bridge between Spirit and our imaginations. The dream state holds that place between the conscious mind and unconscious mind—a place where spirit can talk to us. Some dreams we remember and others we do not.

Dreaming is a common experience for everyone. Generally, dreams reveal our present emotional state and issues requiring our immediate attention and action. They are messages from our own inner self, our guides, our teachers and God. They provide us with insight about what is happening in our everyday life, so pay attention to them.

We have many types of dreams—fun, scary, frustrating, ones that teach and inspire, and ones from the past (in this life and from past lives), present, and future.

When we dream, we travel spiritually out of our body. Remember that we are spiritual beings having a physical experience, and the best way to revisit the spiritual realms is often in the dream state. While our physical body remains safely in our bed, our spiritual self rises up and goes exploring to meet other spirits by way of our imagination, thoughts, and emotions.

At the end of the dream, we always come back to our physical body in that warm bed. So don't worry that you won't return.

We intuitively differentiate the dreaming experience from the final act of dying. In our dream state, we see ourselves in everyday life, in a past life, and in a future life. In the spiritual world, time is an illusion and does not exist. Everything happens simultaneously.

Sometimes our dreams play out as if watching a movie. Many times our dreams deliver messages from our spirit guides, especially when we experience a recurring dream. God and our guides are trying to tell us something, or maybe there is information we need to learn. Sometimes they speak to us using symbols.

For example, if you see yourself riding a bicycle, the meaning behind that could be "you need more balance in your life." Or, you should "balance energies before moving ahead under full steam,"[23] as explained by Betty Bethard, an interpreter of dream symbolization in her book, *The Dream Book, Symbols for Self-Understanding.* There are many books available that can help you explore your dream symbols and the different types of dreams.

Premonition Dreams

These dreams enable us to see into the future and can be a bit disconcerting when we don't understand their significance.

For example, you may visualize yourself talking with your co-workers in a dream about a certain topic. Then the next day you actually have that same exact conversation with them. It can feel scary as you ask yourself why is this happening, especially during the first few occurrences.

However, once you wrap your mind around the emotional experience, be assured and grateful for the gift of premonition, knowing you can see in the past, present, and future, always protected and open to communication between you, your co-workers, and Spirit. Explore and enjoy the wisdom as it reveals itself to you through your premonition dreams. You are ahead of the game the next day with your co-workers, as you have already rehearsed the outcome in your dream state. Be aware and utilize this gift as these normal occurrences play out.

Problem-Solving Dreams

This type of dream is interesting because you set the intent before you go to bed, requesting options and solutions for a particular issue within the dream state. Think of an issue that bothers you, requesting your spirit guides to assist you with your problem. Give details of the problem, requesting solutions and complete recall of the dream upon awakening.

Often the issue dissolves in its importance, because perhaps all you needed was a good night's sleep and change in perspective to let it go. Allow this shift of perspective to play out, as a new approach to the problem and solution reveals itself. Perhaps you are given ideas on how to resolve or release it.

It may take more than one night to completely master the art of manifesting solutions to life's dilemmas. I encourage you to practice this newly discovered power within you to express your intent and wait for the results.

Vivid Dreams

Our dreams come and go and we barely remember them. Occasionally, we experience an extremely vivid and unforgettable dream as if watching a movie animated with color, action, and emotion. As we begin to awaken partially, we relive the dream, expanding even more on the storyline. We have the inner feeling that an important message is being revealed.

When this happens, I encourage you to make every effort to awaken fully enough to write down the whole dream with as much detail as you can remember. Then, upon awakening the next morning, reread it and ponder the message being revealed. Put the writing away for a week or a month and review it again for even more kernels of wisdom. It can be great fun and a powerful way for us to connect with our higher selves, guides, and teachers to gain valuable life-changing insights from our dreams.

Bad Dreams and Frustrating Dreams

Some dreams can be very disturbing and scary. We often project our fears in the dream state—a very safe place to act out our anger, frustrations, and other repressed feelings. In the dream state, we express our emotions freely and openly without someone judging us, so know that it is acceptable to have bad or frustrating dreams, even though you may feel a bit uncomfortable.

For example, I seem to have a recurring bad dream in which I travel to different locations. I am always racing around attempting to get to the airport, bus or train station with too much luggage weighing me down or getting in my way, and I am always late. It is an extremely frustrating dream for me because, in my everyday waking hours, I am always organized, on time, and frequently arriving very early.

I understand the "too much luggage" concept. In reality, I do pack too much stuff. I am sure my frustrating dream of lateness is my higher self subtly suggesting that I decrease my stress and workload, and stop trying to cram so much into a day. I act out my stressful and overworked busyness in my dreams. As I grow older and slow down and pace myself better, it's interesting how that recurring dream seems to have diminished. I finally got the message to slow down and pace myself. Wow! I love it when those "aha" moments arrive.

Nightmares

This type of dream explodes in our minds and bodies with huge amounts and ranges of emotions. This is not a fun experience! Typically, nightmares re-enact a traumatic event or emotion from our current life or even a past-life. We relive the difficult and recurring emotional traumas as if in the present moment. For example, nightmares occur frequently with our troops who go to war. They have witnessed horrific scenes in their waking days that become difficult to assimilate and "turn off" when they go to sleep. They relive those experiences and emotions in the dream state, which poses a huge challenge to manage and overcome.

If you experience horrible nightmares, I recommend that you seek help from your family or a health care provider. Sometimes we require a little extra help on the psychological side of our life, even though we are never alone on the spiritual side.

Lucid Dreams

Have you ever noticed yourself dreaming and you begin to change the outcome of the imagery flowing through your mind? Some say this occurs toward the end of the sleep process as we begin to awaken from the dream state, while others have the ability to remain completely aware during an entire dream. This self-awareness in the dream state is called lucid dreaming.

I have experienced this type of imagery toward the end of frightening dreams where I visualized a different outcome (sometimes even two or three different outcomes) from the original disturbing impressions. Perhaps I am using my gift of imagination and manifestation to shift a negative situation into a positive one.

Many times lucid dreaming manifests solely as complete awareness, knowing we are dreaming without changing outcomes and acting only as observers, while allowing our creative minds to play out our adventures by interacting with our conscious and unconscious minds.

Daydreaming

Take the jump from lucid dreaming and wander into the world called daydreaming, where you are fully awake yet detached from your everyday reality, allowing the mind to drift to imagined altered realities. Perhaps it is a form of mediation or tapping into your imagination and creativity.

I enjoy allowing my mind to wander into a variety of scenarios. For example, I thoroughly enjoy daydreaming as I gaze out my kitchen window each morning and let my mind wander to some faraway place. Many times, I focus on my immediate surroundings. I simply imagine what the world is like for birds visiting the bird feeders and water features scattered throughout my yard.

I observe their world as they take turns at the birdbath, chasing each other, nipping at each other, and splashing as they drink and bathe. I wonder what their family relationships consist of and whether is it strictly survival and instinct driven.

I love watching the mother quail as she guides her babies to the water dish with dad guarding from up above on the tall bush with a watchful eye. I let my imagination run wild as I create a world for them. Perhaps daydreaming bridges my wakeful mind to my spiritual higher mind embellishing and expanding my thoughts, creativity, ambitions, and dreams. What fun!

Back to reality… As we grow up, our dreams change as we change and become more mature and sure of whom we are. We will always dream, even when we are old. God and our spiritual guides and teachers always work with us at deeper levels too, not just in the dream state, since we are in constant communication with them at some level working on whatever lesson moves to the forefront.

Enjoy your dream experiences. They hold the key to the Power of Me. Utilize this key as you peek into your mind and soul every night to gain insight, improve your life, and realize your full potential in your waking hours. Empowerment and wisdom flows to you every night in your dream state. Appreciate and nurture this deep connection and gift from Spirit.

CHAPTER 13

The Power of Intuition: Glimpses of Greater Wisdom

It's in every one of us to be wise. Find your heart, open up both your eyes. We can all know everything without ever knowing why.

It's in every one of us by and by.

– "It's in Every One of Us" by singer/songwriter David Pomeranz

I urge you to learn to trust your intuition and your inner knowingness as you are guided in the direction of your highest good as you flow between your intellect and your innate wisdom.

In your childhood, you were constantly changing emotionally, physically, mentally, and spiritually. You were always going back and forth between periods of equilibrium and disequilibrium.[24] This movement back and forth is necessary to facilitate your growth spurts, but it can also be emotionally and mentally challenging until you can get to a place of maturity and feeling comfortable in your body, as you learn to consciously shift between your intuitive self and your logical, reasoning mind. At times, you may rely too heavily on your logical brain to sort out your external environment and all of its complexities and ignore your inner realm.

Sometimes you may not consciously discover that inner world or comfort level of balance until you are older. For some, it can happen sooner, in their teens and in their twenties, which is one primary reason why I wrote this book—to help you find your true self and the joy in life, hopefully at a much earlier age, and to trust the power of your intuition and subdue that logical-ego personality from worrying whether you are right or wrong.

Now that you are an adult, the searching and learning continues as you explore and expand upon unlimited practical choices including career, education, family, relationships such as marriage or partnerships, children (or not), location of home, health care, travels and more. It is all a push-pull dynamic that creates movement in your life so you can mature as a spiritual being in a physical world, experiencing all that life has to offer.

The important thing is to keep looking within you for the answers on how to live in this physical world called Mother Earth. You have the wisdom already—called intuition. This inner, deep *knowing* motivates you to make choices and respond with a more instinctive "gut feeling," without always rationally understanding them. Learn to trust this inner library of knowing and balance it with your reasoning and logic. Please consider that your intuitive abilities are also connected with your spiritual higher self, so it is important you don't brush aside this intrinsic gift. As we evolve more into the golden age of awakening, we will rely more on our intuitive abilities and less on our ego/rational brains.

As a beginner, one simple tool to refine your intuitive abilities is to ask yourself a few questions. Close your eyes, take a few deep breaths, and ask yourself the following:

- Who am I?
- What is my purpose today?
- What is my purpose in this particular lifetime?
- Am I in the right relationship?

Just *be* with yourself. Go ahead and ask other questions that are on your mind. Wait in silence for the answer. You may need to do this several times before you can distinguish the difference between your own mental thoughts and your intuitive impressions. This is a great skill and gift to develop. Try not to doubt the intuitive voice you hear with the answers to the logical questions you seek. Have a pen and paper ready to write down your answers or use a recording device. You can use this technique, one of many, throughout your life to help you differentiate, as well as blend your instinctive intuition with your logical mind.

Our lives are full of demands to do things that keep us trapped in an unending cycle of externally focused activities. We are preoccupied by our need to accomplish our goals in the outer world continually relying on our left-brain logical mind instead of our right-brain creative and instinctive mind. By focusing our attention on our inner world and cultivating our connection to the spiritual realm through meditation, we can expend less effort, yet accomplish much more through the practice of being present. When we employ our intuition and inner knowing, we are guided in the direction of our greatest good. One of the most important challenges we encounter is learning to trust this guidance.

Learning to *be* with yourself, instead of primarily concentrating on *doing*, uplifts you to a place of peace and balance. Learning to *be* present is probably more important than all the things I thought I needed to *do*. This concept was difficult for me to learn. Ignoring my intuition, and so busy running around *doing* everyday activities, I frequently forgot to just *be* and listen to my higher self's inner-wisdom, intermingled with the voice of spirit and the power within me.

Along the way, you may need guidance. I encourage you to ask for help from Spirit or from loved ones. Don't keep it all inside of you as you meet the challenges of your life. Find a trusted confidante to share your thoughts with, or keep a personal journal of your inner reflections.

Here is an example of how I intertwined my logical life goals with my intuition. Many people throughout their life feel stuck and can't intuitively discover their purpose, and are unsure of the questions and responses or simply feel lost. In my younger years, I frequently felt unable to know the questions, let alone answer them. I grappled with figuring out my college major long before I asked: "What is my purpose in life?"

Confused and unsure of myself, I began by logically setting minor goals and transitioned from one step to the next, while keeping an open mind. I continually monitored and shifted my perspective if I became discouraged or lost hope.

In my early college days, I knew my goal was a Bachelor of Arts degree but wasn't sure about my major. Frequently, I felt lost and sometimes discouraged, yet, I continued to enroll in all the basic classes needed to complete the requirements for the degree.

While attending college, I needed to take the next transitional step and seek a part-time job. Even though seven months pregnant (ignoring the fact that it could be an obstacle), I applied for an advertising sales job at the college newspaper for the fall quarter, not realizing at the time how synchronicity (and my intuition) were aligning me with my potential major in journalism. All was in perfect order, as I listened to my subtle inner voice and gut feelings leading me from one step to the next.

I enrolled in a variety of majors, scrutinizing what matched with my goal. I continued to move forward, rationally reviewing my choices and options, until I received a spark of insight and heard my intuitive voice telling me that the journalism degree was perfect for me. Afterwards, I marveled at the way everything magically fell into place as I utilized and balanced both my intuitive and reasoning abilities.

Allow patience, tenacity, and perseverance with a dash of spontaneity to shift your perspective if you feel lost or stuck. Make a list of the positives and negatives in your life and see if you can shift your thoughts away from the negative ones. Most importantly, do not give up on yourself. Trust your intuition and your inner voice, knowing you are always at the right place at the right time.

My perseverance rewarded me with a new direction, as my inner drive, intuition and fear of boredom encouraged me to find the answers. There were many challenging times when I became stuck in a rut, due to a lack of motivation and confidence in myself. We can easily fall into the comfort of a routine and allow anxiety, doubt, depression, and fear of change freeze us in time.

In those moments, I strived to change my outlook, knowing it was the most effective way out of my rut. I would examine my job, my relationships, and extracurricular activities and logically analyze how I was spending my NOW time. Did my life flow or did I need to make adjustments, allowing the possibilities, creative ideas or images unfold, as I quietly listened to my intuitive voice?

Make a commitment to yourself that today is the day you will consciously start with new, fresh ideas and get rid of the old stale ones. Redefine your desires, needs and goals. Use the power of self-responsibility, manifestation, and intuition to create what you want in life, by stating your new intention and taking the appropriate steps to achieve your goal, while surrendering to this process. Open up the space to plan, assimilate and integrate your new prospects by lifting yourself out of the heavy energies of doubt, fear, frustration, guilt, sadness, depression, etc., and acknowledge all the things in your life that are working and that you are grateful for.

Tapping into your power of gratitude shifts you inward, in order to hear your intuitive inner voice. As you nurture, center and restore yourself, you will experience an alignment with a higher frequency of vibrations where new creative options will be revealed to you by spirit. If you notice yourself falling back into old patterns, floundering or resisting the changes, decide to choose positive forward movement. Only you can utilize the power of choice. It is up to you to determine the best evolutionary course to follow.

Acknowledging the wonderful gift and spiritual tool of intuition carries you one step closer to your heart and soul, your true inner God-self. Integration of your intuition and reasoning with your life experiences equals success, confidence, creativity and access to a greater wisdom.

CHAPTER 14

Angels, Teachers, Guides and Over-Souls

Learn to get in touch with the silence within yourself and know that everything in this life has a purpose; there are no mistakes, no coincidences. All events are blessings given to us to learn from.

– Elisabeth Kübler-Ross

All of us have guardian angels at our side, inspiring our life's journey forward with joy and gusto, as they whisper many options and choices in our ears to strive for the best we can be.

These angels, as referenced by a variety of names in different cultures and traditions, are our constant motivators, protectors, and companions, gently nudging and guiding us as we weave around our preplanned path, according to our contracts, always engaging in the use of free will and free choice. Throughout the many stages of our lives, we have a variety of angels who choose to take on the role of guides and teachers, both physical and non-physical, to inspire and assist us. For simplicity's sake, I will call them guides.

When contemplating non-physical angels or guides, I am referring to etheric, spiritual, or celestial beings. In referencing physical angels or guides, I envision interactive relationships with our family, friends, co-workers, etc., in a physical body. They support us as our guides and teachers, also.

As we evolve and mature through the various stages of our current lifetime, our non-physical spiritual guides vary as our lessons alter, modify, and shift. When we are children, we have guides who help us through the birth cycle and our early years as we progress through our many stages of childhood.

In adulthood, we evolve and mature through several stages of growth and our guides change as we change. We have one main spiritual guide or teacher, who is with us throughout eternity. I think of this main guide as the head manager, synchronizing all lifetimes, on all planes of existence and at all levels and dimensions, referred to as our "**Over-Soul.**"[25*] This main spiritual guide manages all of our lifetimes simultaneously.

Since time does not exist in the spiritual world, but only in the physical Third-Dimensional world, everything, including our past, present, and future, are all occurring simultaneously. We are living in an eternal moment, which we experience as "now." Amazing thought, is it not? The children being born now understand this concept.

The older generations, previously existing with a denser vibratory rate, moved at a slower pace, mainly choosing to plan for their future and reminisce about the past. Currently, the vibratory rate and energy levels have accelerated to such a heightened state, that even the older ones feel more awareness of the present moment. Frequently, living for today becomes our only option.

Our Over-Soul manages all the higher selves (which is the true soul essence and many aspects of us) in each of the different lifetimes, and our guides work with each of our higher selves so that we progress in each lifetime to learn our necessary lessons. Let's take a look at each of these concepts individually.

The **higher self** in this lifetime on earth is our true essence and an aspect of, or part of, our whole spiritual self. As mentioned earlier, we are spiritual beings having a physical experience. Our spiritual self or higher self is always with us and remembers everything from every lifetime, whether in the physical or non-physical realm. It assists and guides us through our current lifetime.

We also have non-physical **spiritual guides** who will gently nudge us to be in the right place at the right time, so we can experience certain lessons to fulfill our **lifetime contract**. As noted, within our lifetime contract, we choose what lessons we will learn. This was all decided before we were born and agreed upon between our Over-Soul, our higher self, guides, our God, and us. Our guides will assist us in fulfilling these lessons always in alignment with our free will.

For example, imagine you are walking down the street and unsure which way to turn—right or left. Your spiritual guide or higher self can suggest that you turn right (prompted as a thought in your head), since you will meet the person with whom you will share an experience so that both of you can learn a particular lesson as outlined in each of your current lifetime contracts.

You may choose to turn left instead, (since you always have free will) and you may miss the opportunity to meet this person now. That is all right. Your guide will find another way to give you another opportunity on another day to meet this person. You will still fulfill your contract at some point, as you had planned, before you were born. It just may take a bit longer if you choose the opposite way your higher self and guides suggest.

The above brief description is just one possible scenario for this current lifetime on Planet Earth. The same happens simultaneously in every lifetime, since time doesn't really exist.

See the chart below for a graphic description of the concept of Over-Soul and how it relates to each lifetime.

Over-Soul

Lifetime #1 ________________________________ higher self
Lifetime #2 ________________________________ higher self
Lifetime #3 ________________________________ higher self
Lifetime #4 ________________________________ higher self

(Your lifetimes continue for eons of time, and will be managed by your Over-Soul, that is also a part of you.)

From this diagram you can see that the Over-Soul oversees each of your lifetimes. Using time for clarification purposes, one lifetime, for example, exists in the past, one co-exists in the present, and two are in the future. Each lifetime positions one of your higher selves (each an aspect of your soul) in place, the true essence of you, assisting you to manage your experiences according to your contract.

I discovered that the spiritual, non-physical guides direct my experiences from a much larger perspective viewing my Akashic Records of many lifetimes and my current agreed upon contract from a much broader viewpoint than I can comprehend at my current level of spiritual maturity.

While in the duality of Planet Earth, we tend to be "veiled" and cannot always see or understand the larger scheme of a higher reality. "Veil" means that we agreed in this lifetime to be born forgetting our true essence so that we could fully understand duality, to see if we could, in fact, find our way back to the light, to our true selves, and back home to God.

Expanding your perspective and observing your interactions, reactions, thoughts, words, and choices becomes the source of your power. Making conscious choices with the whispers of support from your guides is your path to true empowerment. You remain the driver of your current car with the inner knowledge to *know* if you should turn right or left, with the assistance of your guides playing the role of the "back seat driver," gently suggesting and nudging you to make the correct choice at the precise and correct moment. Go within for a moment here, close your eyes, take a few deep breaths, and feel your inner strength and empowerment as you drive your car down the highway of life.

Some of us will successfully walk the path back home in this lifetime; others will not. There is no time limitation in the evolutionary process. Everyone will soar to the top of the mountain, sprout angel wings, and make it back home eventually.

One more note about the above diagram. Sometimes life drifts into uncharted and challenging territory because you may not always understand a particular lesson. There is such a thing as *bleed-through*, in which the activities of another lifetime merge into this lifetime and you feel or see them. You may be confused and not be able to comprehend their significance. You may need to breathe through this experience, and say "Oh well," realizing that this is another one of those mysteries in your life.

Ask your spiritual guide to reveal its meaning for you in this lifetime. Eventually, you will be given the answer you seek, whether in a dream or meditation, or possibly one of your physical guides will drop the answer in your lap one day in the middle of a conversation. Be aware and chuckle to yourself, knowing your guides and teachers have just answered your question.

I am continually in awe when such synchronizations occur. These unexpected events are a cosmic gift emphasizing our close connection with the divine. They present us with an instantaneous opportunity to experience a higher moment of consciousness, where we receive validation of our ability to commune with our Creator.

It's important to differentiate between our spiritual guides and other entities; those departed souls who have decided to stay close to the earth plane, rather than moving into the light. Our spiritual guides are here to love and serve. Entities usually are not present to assist you, but rather, to help themselves since they usually are lost or perhaps have an unresolved issue.

As mentioned in Chapter 11, so-called spooks or ghosts can be mischievous and even disruptive by not realizing they are overstepping their bounds. I remind you to use the tools I suggested to gently ask the entity to leave or even seek outside assistance, if necessary, to facilitate its removal. You will know the difference between a disruptive entity and your loving spiritual guides and teachers.

Many years ago I learned this valuable lesson. One of the houses I lived in for years always felt uncomfortable. I blamed it on the constant remodeling and repairs the house required. One day I saw an apparition, in the form of a man, sitting in my chair in my bedroom, grotesquely laughing at me as if in a drunken state. He scared me and made me feel very uneasy. By this time, we were in the process of moving and attempting to sell the house, with much resistance for at least two years. I tried my best on my own to rid this entity from my home.

Finally, I sought outside assistance and called two psychic friends who came over and helped me rid the entity from my home. One month later the house sold. I share this story not to create doubt or fear but to differentiate the two essences. You may experience both, yet each requires different approaches. Trust you will know the difference. Use love as your guide. If it feels right, embrace it; if not, change it.

In this lifetime, the people and even animals we meet are all physical guides and teachers acting as mirrors on this plane of existence. Some of them come into our lives for a brief moment and others stay our entire lifetime, such as our parents, our brothers and sisters, husbands and wives, our own children, and even our pets.

The same principles outlined above for non-physical guides, also apply to physical guides, as you perceive them with your five senses in the flesh. They stand before you, difficult to miss, since they come into your life for a specific reason to teach you something or for you to teach them. We continuously pivot between the roles of teacher and student. The everyday interactions and dramas you have with each other are actually you playing out your karma and contractual agreements.

Again, how will you relate to your fellow actors? Will you choose to continue with the karma or create new dramas, or will you choose a way to clear the old wounds and move to a place of transformation always interacting with love, light, free will, and balance?

Know you have both physical and non-physical guides with you at all times. You just need to ask for guidance and listen for the answers. They will counsel, love, support, and nurture you, always in alignment with your highest good. Accept the idea that you are not alone and that spiritual guidance is there waiting for you to hear their soft whispers. Take some time each day and listen for the whisper.

CHAPTER 15

Conversations with Your Spirit Guides

So I say to you, ask, and it will be given to you; search, and you will find; knock and the door will be opened for you.

– Jesus Christ

How do you meet your spiritual non-physical guides or listen for their whispers? You request to speak with them, using the question-and-answer technique as described earlier. This process, although easy, takes practice. You may not get a response right away, but keep asking, listening and looking for the acknowledgement. It comes in many forms; from the answer flowing directly into your mind, or the book that literally falls off the bookshelf into your hands containing the reply you are looking for. You could also run into a physical guide, an old friend, who starts talking about the very topic you have been contemplating. Synchronicity plays a big role here. Things seem to fall into place.

To start, go into a meditative state by relaxing in a comfortable position.

Usually, it is best to sit straight in a comfortable chair, with your feet on the floor uncrossed and hands sitting comfortably in your lap, or you can lie down, (as long as you don't fall asleep).

Close your eyes, take three deep breaths and release any tension in your body. If your mind wanders, gently bring your focus back to breathing and relaxing. Then, ask your guides to come to you. Ask them their names and what they would like you to know today. Carry on a conversation with them. It is important you realize you must ask for what you desire. Always honoring free will and free choice, your guides will not respond otherwise.

Sometimes, I like to pose a question by writing it out, and then type or write the answer as it comes to me. I listen intently, transcribing the first image or words that I receive. I don't question it or analyze it. I don't go back and reread it. I allow the words to flow.

Sometimes, you can say hello to your guides or to God. You may get a "hello" as an answer. At other times, you may want to sit back and relax without asking any questions and simply listen. Your guides, God, or even your higher self may begin speaking to you as you remain in a receptive state.

If I am not sure who is speaking, I ask. Or I may just listen and not concern myself with who is speaking. At times, you will get no answer—only silence. This can be frustrating, especially if you are new to this process, but keep asking and listening. It may not be time yet for you to know the information you are seeking.

Some people may discount this process and will say it is "just your imagination. That can't possibly be voices from your spiritual guides." They may give you a wary look, suspecting you may be delusional, as they make judgments from the logical side of their brain. There may be times when your unconscious mind plays back something you heard from someone else. These experiences can be a bit confusing, especially in the beginning. Challenge yourself and continue to practice. Eventually, you will learn to distinguish your guide's voice from your own inner voice or even from your chattering ego. Definitely ignore the person who tells you "it is just your imagination." Tell that inexperienced soul that you love exploring your imagination! It opens up a whole new world of knowledge for you, and gently suggest he or she do the same, (unless you suspect some form of psychological disorder. If so, I encourage medical guidance).

Some people believe we can speak to our guides, loved ones who have passed on, animals, birds, bugs or rocks. In her book on communicating with animals, [26] author and animal intuitive Maia Kinkaid uses the question-and-answer techniques. She has received many beautiful stories and messages from the nature kingdom.

In their *Book of Stones,*[27] authors, Robert Simmons and Naisha Ahsian, listen to the rocks and intuitively receive their messages of wisdom and healing. Our libraries, bookstores, and websites are filled with several books and theories on conversing with our spiritual guides using meditation to quiet the mind, the question-and-answer techniques, as well as many types of soothing music that will help you get into a relaxed, receptive state.

Remember, there are no accidents. If a book falls off the shelf into your hands, chances are one of your guides is trying very hard to get your attention, suggesting very strongly that you have magically manifested a book you should read, one filled with delight and fun or one filled with important, serious information for your current stage of growth. When things like that happen, definitely take action and read the book. Our guides are not always obvious in their efforts to communicate with us, and generally use less conspicuous methods.

Once in a while, I will see a sign in the window of a bookstore promoting a book, which strongly attracts my attention. I usually feel this attraction or resonation as a tightening or swirling in my heart or chest area. I respond intuitively to my inner voice and guides, knowing this is a book I should read.

Many times, I will sit in meditation and ask a question and not really get an answer, as I mentioned earlier. Then a month or two later, I pick up a book or magazine article and there it is, the answer to my question. I just laugh quietly to myself and thank my spiritual guidance.

The point to all of this is to establish a relationship and a dialog with your higher self, your guides, and God. You will be amazed by the miraculous experiences that enter your life, as a result of this connection to the spiritual realm. The realization that you are never truly alone is a profound one. What a blessing to recognize that we are protected and guided along our path in life. Nothing is an accident; you planned it all in your pre-birth contract with yourself.

Fully comprehending the love and protection I feel, knowing that my spiritual guidance oversees the path before me, is very comforting and reassuring. When I first learned of spiritual guides, I felt awestruck and fascinated by the concept. I would like to share an experience I had with a spiritual guide, which reassured me of their existence. The first time I telepathically heard this spirit's voice in my mind, it brought tears to my eyes, as I recognized and felt the essence of a recently departed family member. I vividly remember, as I gazed at an old family video of him, hearing him whisper in my ear, "I am right here. I am right here." I then burst out crying because I missed this person so much, but I could also hear him as if he was sitting next to me in his physical form.

I heard him speak in a soft, reassuring voice so clearly, that I couldn't question his authenticity. I then realized that this family member died at an early age so he could guide me, and probably other family members, from the spiritual realm rather than from the physical. This confirmation and guidance became his purpose and his gift. What an incredibly beautiful and magical moment he shared with me. I encourage you to transform your life, by opening up to this wonderful gift from the angelic kingdom.

Begin now, using the question-and-answer technique, or whatever works for you, to empower your conversations with your spiritual guides and see where it leads. Understanding, deep down, that you have this spiritual guidance with you throughout your life will help you live from a place of trust and wisdom rather than from that confused, indecisive dialog in your head, questioning if you are right, or if you are making the proper choices and decisions. Acknowledge and trust the whispers of encouragement and inner-knowledge from your spiritual guides as they accompany you on your journey to spiritual awakening and enlightenment, always in alignment with love, light, free will and balance.

CHAPTER 16

Empathy, Love, and Loving Too Much

Love one another, but make not a bond of love:
Let it rather be a moving sea between the shores of your souls.

– KAHLIL GIBRAN

"What is this incredible sadness I feel inside today?" I asked myself. I almost felt as though I could just curl up and cry from deep within my soul.

Some days, I cry a little and it helps to relieve the stress, tension, and pain I feel in the pit of my stomach. Other times I sob and do not always understand why. What I do know is that some of these tears are not mine. As an empath, I feel so much of other people's emotional baggage.

What, exactly, is an empath? The dictionary defines *empathy* as "the capacity for participating in the feelings or ideas of another." I view empathy as a gift; a wonderful ability to feel the other person's emotions whether love, compassion, hate, or anger. An empath feels the full range of emotions, both the pleasant and unpleasant. The unpleasant emotions challenge me, and can be difficult until I sort out my feelings from some other source.

Some people are empaths; yet remain unaware of the dynamics of empathy. They begin to believe there is something wrong with them. They may question themselves and their sanity, since they perceive odd emotions overtaking them and are unsure why they feel the way they do. I reacted and responded this way for many years.

"Why am I depressed? Why is it so hard to be in large crowds of people and come away feeling totally drained of all my energy? Why do I feel like I want to cry for no reason?" These represent some of the questions I asked myself.

It took me years to unravel my emotions. I needed to differentiate what feelings were mine versus the emotions of others. This did not pose an easy task, especially since I did not have a spiritual teacher within my physical realm to guide me in my younger years. It is definitely not taught in school. In my mid-thirties, I began to awaken, understand, and open up to the influence of my higher self or soul-self. This also meant I was becoming even more sensitive than before.

I would like to share some tips on how to know, understand, and live with this very special gift and, most importantly, how to accept the responsibility that comes with it.

First, once you realize and understand that you possess the gift of empathy and you sort out your emotions, this awareness gives birth to an expansion of your psychic abilities and sense of empowerment. You will intuitively know what to do in a variety of situations, and through this, you develop more confidence. Other people will come to you, trusting you with their personal stories, without knowing why they feel compelled to tell you. You will notice frequent, uneasy sensations in crowds of people prompting you, for example, to park your car near an exit, in case you need to make a quick getaway from an uncomfortable setting. In addition, you will be acutely aware and sensitive to physical and emotional pain, while remaining attentive to the sensations originating from other people.

These experiences can be painful and challenging, yet also rewarding once you comprehend and accept this powerful gift of empathy. Many emotions are enjoyable and beautiful too. While walking in nature, you immediately tune into the calming, loving vibrations of the wildlife, plants and rocks surrounding you in this nurturing environment. For example, I marvel at the gentle pulsing I sense from holding a crystal in my hand as we mutually communicate love to each other.

Second, we cannot save others even when we feel their pain. We accept the responsibility only for our own emotions, actions, and reactions. We cannot take on the drama of others and think we benefit them. In truth, we are not assisting; we are hindering the choices of another by stepping over their personal boundaries as *loving too much*. Our overabundance of love, concern, and reaction to another's drama creates an imbalance because we give away a part of ourselves—our power. In the early stages of our empathic awareness, the imbalance of loving too much frequently becomes an issue.

We must allow others to experience life and learn from their mistakes. It is difficult to watch our loved ones suffer through life without offering assistance. We already feel what they are going through; that is enough. I encourage you to stand back and exhibit *unconditional love* by allowing them to experience their own adventures without expectations.

Third, we can facilitate another's healing process, but we cannot do it for them. We are not healers. (The key word here is "facilitate," which means, "to make easier.") For example, I would meditate to send healing energy to the earth after a natural disaster. I do this with the intention of providing my thoughts, intentions of love, and therapeutic energy to facilitate the earth in her healing process. Mother Earth chooses for herself if she will use that thought of love and healing. I cannot heal her; I can only offer support. At least knowing that we can facilitate the healing process allows us the satisfaction of doing something to help, even if it is on a spiritual level rather than at an emotional/mental/physical one.

Fourth, we can feel all of life and stay open to both the positive and the negative, but we must keep our boundaries strong so the negative energies do not bring us down. We learn what is ours and what is not. See Chapter 11 to review the grounding, clearing, protecting and balancing techniques to help us firm up our boundaries and bring ourselves back to balance.

I cannot emphasize enough how valuable these techniques are for bringing you back to your place of centeredness. Take the time to incorporate them, along with quiet meditation, to renew your inner power, maintain your boundaries, and identify and release your feelings.

Also, clear and replenish your personal energy field by requesting your higher self, God or Mother Earth to facilitate your process by refilling you with healing energy. Feel it flow and permeate your whole being with loving, restorative, and harmonizing energy.

One quick way to clear your energy field is simply to rinse your hands under running water for a few minutes, especially if you feel drained and sluggish after an outing among crowds of people. Better yet, soak your whole body in an Epsom salt bath; since it clears your auric field and will make you feel relaxed and revitalized.

I incorporate these simple tools into my life when experiencing reduced physical vitality or depressed moods. After completion, I feel refreshed and back to my true self again. I encourage you to practice using these tools and find others that are perfect for you.

Over the years, I encountered many opportunities to discover and fine-tune my empathic abilities. My very first vivid experience of my empathic gift occurred many years ago, when I visited a new art gallery in town that featured beautiful pieces of stone art, mainly crystals, displayed as artistic sculptures. As I walked around the gallery, I began to feel very uncomfortable and dizzy. I sensed that some of these stones were very unhappy. Ripped from the earth and cut with the intention of using them as superficial commercial art instead of gifts for natural healing, the stones' energy reflected the anguish of their newly forced role.

Please understand this is how I interpreted this situation. I felt something was wrong and started to hyperventilate. I could not catch my breath. I had to leave the gallery quickly. It took me about half an hour to catch my breath and restore my balance again.

I am not saying we should not admire and own the beautiful stones. On the contrary, they should be loved, honored and displayed in our homes, healing centers, and businesses. I suggest that we simply appreciate that they are living beings and need to be respected for the gifts and treasures they reveal.

They each have a purpose and express their life force energetically, which explains why I felt uncomfortable in the art gallery. This incident, as my first conscious perception of energy, demonstrates how I detected the emotional energy and vibration of an object. Most of the time, I do not experience such clarity or always comprehend such occurrences. I still wonder to this day the reason for my intense reaction to the stones. Were they really unhappy or did the huge volume of stones in one place elevate my newly expanded sensitivities? I may never know, but I embrace this vivid and unforgettable lesson in empathy.

According to my parents, another episode happened when I was only six months old. I was sleeping in my crib in an upstairs bedroom when my uncle passed away downstairs. At the very moment of his death, I started screaming. I must have felt my uncle dying, or his fear of transitioning. I do not have any memory of this event, or any understanding of why he frightened me. I may never know. The point is that I demonstrated empathic behavior as an infant. Even though I don't remember the event, I can sense the memory of him in my body at the time of his death.

Another example would be the intense emotion I feel from my own father. He endured the last days of World War II as a prisoner of war during which he suffered from severe starvation and was near death. After three months of captivity and weighing only 106 pounds, the stress and agony of torture, stomach ailments, injuries, and frozen feet, created horrific physical and emotional trauma as he confronted his own mortality, watching his friends die one after the other.

This man, living in post-traumatic stress syndrome after his horrific war experience, raised me. It took him years to be able to talk about his trauma and flashbacks without breaking down into tears.

I deeply felt all of his pain throughout my childhood, and, as a result, became an anti-war advocate since I had already endured the atrocities of war.

Having vicariously felt the pain of war, I could not understand why anyone would want to injure or end the life of another. It has always been a simple and probably naïve answer for me; all parties must simply agree to lay down their guns and never use them again.

If we were all empaths or more evolved souls, this could easily be accomplished. However, from my perspective, that is not the case at this time in our history because many reject (consciously or unconsciously) the concept of the spiritual connection of ONENESS while immersed in this physical matrix of illusion. I believe that if we hurt one person, we only hurt ourselves by extension.

I still honor our troops and the parents who send their children to war. It is my hope that no parent will face such a decision again and that we will end all wars on this planet. These experiences brought to the surface my empathic abilities long before I could verbalize or comprehend the significance of this gift that many of us share.

As an empath, I feel other people's emotions, yet I firmly know deep within myself, that with love, compassion, empathy, and oneness, we will eventually achieve peace on our beloved planet.

As I reflect on our Mother Earth's suffering, I hope she will reveal with utmost clarity and intensity, what she feels so that everyone will finally understand! We are witnessing the earth changes very clearly now. Our Mother Earth has been holding on, to protect all life on our planet, but she is losing the battle. We are all losing the battle. We cannot keep treating the earth and all her finite resources as possessions to use and throw away like garbage.

As another example, I vividly remember and sensed the pain from the Gulf of Mexico oil spill in 2010 when the BP Petroleum Company broke an artery in the core of the earth and the heart of the ocean at a depth of 5,000 feet. For months, oil gushed from this site, causing irreparable damage to wildlife, the environment, and the local economies.

With this disaster and other climate changes, we have now reached a precarious point. As the Hopi prophecy suggests, we are at a crossroads. We can change our ways for the good of all or we can destroy our earth and ourselves. What do we choose?

With the many earth changes happening with our planet and all of her inhabitants, a weakness and despondency frequently overcomes me, and I feel as though I have nothing more to give.

I try to remain mindful of my inner strength to meditate and send my gifts of love and light to all of Mother Earth to support her at this pivotal point. The action of giving back in this fashion gives me an outlet for sharing my gifts.

Looking back, I wonder if the oil spill and my father's war experience offer a demonstration of duality in action and an opportunity to clear old karma and suffering. I acknowledge this perspective as I empathically endure the experiences deep within my soul. As I feel the pain, do I also participate in the clearing of the old karma? My sense is that I do facilitate the clearing and healing, as I participate in this demonstration of releasing the old karmic lessons of the few, to bring in the new waves of love for the collective. I continue the search for clarity.

These types of experiences reverberate throughout my body, heart, and soul, from a place of compassion and love. As an empath, I need to take care of myself by replenishing my own energy fields. Giving to others is easier for me; however, I find it challenging to pause and care for myself. Where is that place of balance between giving and receiving—between loving and loving too much?

I believe this imbalance manifests as a prevalent issue for many of us, particularly with empaths. The discomfort I hold in the pit of my stomach (above my belly button) is where I perceive emotion, expressing as my power center. For you, it could manifest in your heart or lower abdominal area.

Many times the imbalance reveals itself as tightness or a swirling motion in my solar plexus area, just above my belly button. This sensation can be so intense that I react by doubling over in pain. This power center also emerges as an entry point or an emotional meter for my intuition—my inner knowing where I discern at a physical and emotional level if something is right or wrong.

I have spent my whole life bearing other people's emotions by participating in their karma as well as my own; a very challenging burden I have placed on myself. As previously mentioned, I consider empathy a gift of love and compassion. I have carried others' emotions because I love them.

I have figured out, however, that this love is a bit misdirected and out of balance at times. I give love to others, but do not love myself enough to stay grounded in my own personal power. I need to remind myself that my love is my power, a wonderful lesson I learned from Sharon McErlane's books. [28]

It is a universal love that we all have, if we look for it in ourselves. I forgot to look for my *own* love and my *own* emotions within me. I had everybody's emotions, including my own, all jumbled into one big mess. No wonder I walked through life frustrated, angry, sad, and sometimes physically ill. Occasionally, I would remember how to take care of myself and remain in balance.

For example, as a massage therapist, I would suddenly feel a pain somewhere in my body while administering a treatment to a client. Knowing it did not belong to me, I would say to the pain, "Thank you for the gift of revealing the pain and showing yourself to me." I would then flick my fingers into the air and say, "Pain, leave my physical body now." I would visualize it dissipating into the ethers and the pain would then leave. It was fascinating how that worked. I could hold to my own personal power and boundaries when I was practicing massage, but under other circumstances, it was more difficult not to pick up other people's energies as if I was a vacuum cleaner or a sponge.

I also think it is extremely challenging to keep myself separate from the feelings of family members because the emotional attachments run so deep. No wonder I would wake up some mornings feeling like I had a huge weight around my shoulders. I was carrying around this giant heavy sack of "emotional baggage" that was not mine to carry. I have now realized it is time to shift all the negative emotions and transform them into a positive, loving place of compassion and peace. I choose to come back to my present moment and refuse to fall prey to the emotional drama and regain my sense of self.

"I am done! It is released." The power of my aspirations and expressing my desired outcomes makes it so. It really is that easy once you fully practice and master the art of intention.

When I am overwhelmed, I am eventually pushed to my breaking point where I say, "Enough!" I re-establish my boundaries, detach and re-center myself, and, I then return to my joyful, loving, sensitive self. Of course, I may have to put myself to bed for a day or so, go out into nature, dip into a pool of water, or spend time alone to rejuvenate. I let family members know what is going on so they don't worry or think that I am sick. I simply explain that I need some space and time alone for a while.

When an empath loves too much, they do not allow others to learn from their experiences in life or from their own mistakes. We love that child, mother, husband, or wife so much, that we are willing to take on their emotions, their karma, and even try to "fix them." Empaths misinterpret emotional sharing as an expression of their compassionate assistance, instead of recognizing their actions as an attempt to avoid dealing with their own feelings and needs. When we tend to give too much to others, we block self-love and nourishment for ourselves.

Setting limits on our empathic behavior is necessary to our health and well-being. Remembering to express our own feelings, honestly and openly, with trustworthy friends or loved ones, or through creative self-expression, helps us to maintain a balanced emotional state. Nurturing ourselves by doing things we love, promotes a sense of joy, happiness and peace. We feel energized when we treat ourselves the same way we treat our best friends, with kindness, gentleness and love.

Empathetic people have a tendency to avoid dealing with their own feelings and needs by over-indulging in care giving with those they treasure. This tendency to solve other people's problems or to try to change them for the better can stem from a lack of self-worth. Their sub-conscious belief that they don't deserve love is often the result of a traumatic and abusive childhood. This attitude of unworthiness and craving for love can cause an empath to attempt to prove their value to others through over-giving to the point of exhaustion. Some empaths have a highly advanced ability to read the emotions of others, which they developed at a young age, as a way to compensate and survive in a hostile environment.

When an empath becomes deeply absorbed in resolving the emotional struggles of another, they forget that too much help can become a hindrance. They deprive the other person of the opportunity to learn and grow. They also deny that person the experience of empowerment and sense of accomplishment inherent in successfully overcoming life's emotional conflicts and challenges.

When you permit this to happen, you actually drain yourself and prevent others from experiencing their own emotions; you deprive them of the opportunity to fulfill their own lifetime contracts.

Step back and observe your interactions from a larger perspective. Simply tell the other person: "I love you so much for who you are; I love the truth of you, that I want you to play out your own life's emotions. I can't do it for you, since I would be denying you your opportunity to grow. It is not healthy for me to do this because it drains me of my power and my life force." (Note: you will say this to yourself in private, not face-to-face to the family member. Just project the intention.)

Perhaps you can also incorporate an imagery technique, in which you imagine your spiritual self connecting with the other person's higher self, visualizing the two of you sitting face to face, expressing your loving intentions and desired outcomes. It is my understanding that this technique allows for more clarity at the spiritual level without ego getting in the way.

Your unconditional love for this person has not changed; only the original expectations and obligations you placed on him or her have gone away releasing the need to "fix" them. You love this person for who he or she is, no matter how badly he or she acts. When the conditions soften and melt away, you are free to love openly and genuinely, without feeling obligations or expectations. Eliminate the burden of expectations (which is so much easier said than done).

As you advance this process with someone you love, (for example, your sister), you will begin to notice a change in her behavior. It may be difficult, at first, because she senses something has changed and doesn't like that you are not absorbing and engaging in her issues any longer. She will start misbehaving even more and lashing out at you to continue with the drama you once played.

Hold yourself to your own power and strength. Think of yourself as a mom or dad. Discipline yourself to avoid carrying her emotions and issues so the child will learn the correct behavior and self-responsibility for herself.

We say "no" to the child and mean it. We can't back down. Play with this concept. Experiment with the variables of the interaction to gain clarity. You may come up with your own ideas that serve you better.

Always follow your own intuition that embraces the power and truth of you. Get to know yourself as an empath. It truly is a gift of love and compassion even though you may consider it a curse at times. Love yourself for being the empathic healer that you are. You are facilitating the healing process for yourself, for your family members, co-workers, and friends, for all of mankind, and for our Mother Earth. Give and receive love equally and unconditionally. Beloved, it is quite an assignment God gave us and we agreed to do it!

These types of scenarios have happened to me several times in my life. I seem to have phases when I am humming along in a state of equilibrium. Then something changes in my life to set me off balance—into disequilibrium, and I forget who I am and what my truth is. Along comes another life lesson. Some of us call these "Clearing Opportunities." We release the old challenges and bring in the new possibilities.

I share my experiences with you so you will understand that it is not a bad thing to be an empath. It can become a burden when you are in the middle of your lesson, but eventually you will figure out who you truly are. Sometimes it can take a lifetime of clearing opportunities, because we go through many stages of growth.

Similar to toddlers developing and growing through the many stages of babyhood, experiencing their "terrible two" moments, we continue to evolve all the way into adulthood. We never stop learning, developing or transforming.

If my words and my experiences help you to understand the process better, let you know you are not the only one struggling with this, and that you are not going crazy, then I have accomplished what I set out to do. I believe that as I develop, learn more about who I am, define my truth, and stand in my own empowerment, collectively, we reach a point in time where we learn the same lesson together, because we are all connected. As I evolve and clear, so do you, and the rest of humanity as well. We are all one!

CHAPTER 17

The Sacred Relationship Bridge

You must love in such a way that the person you love feels free.

– Thich Nhat Hanh

"Love, love, love. All you need is love!"

Perhaps you're not old enough to remember that famous Beatles' song, but it's still a popular tune echoing one of the most widely held universal truths by most people around the world. "Love is all you need," right?

The fundamental nature of an empowered, healthy human relationship portrays a connection and bonding of love between two essences in all its actions, inactions and interactions. That's why we need to embrace our sacred relationships as we open our hearts and bond to the power and strength of unconditional love.

Can you comprehend the aspect of strength within this love as you erect a *relationship bridge* of mutual independence, interdependence, and empowerment?

I sense that a transformation has been triggered recently in all of us since adult relationships are more openly and honestly expressed with a variety of distinctive, limitless attributes. A woman loves a man; a man loves a woman; a woman loves a woman; a man loves a man.

I recently noticed several examples of animals forming friendships among different breeds, such as a cat befriending a crow, a goat befriending a horse, and a dolphin befriending a dog. What a beautiful vision to witness relationships in which humans and animals deeply bond, express love and friendship beyond boundaries, instincts, traditions, old mores, and expectations— true expressions of unconditional love.

During this time of the Great Awakening, our boundaries seem to be blurring more and more into love, compassion, truth, and integrity without expectations of separateness according to our designated roles and groupings. Yet, as this transformation unfolds, our relationships continue to morph into the old patterns of separation, acting in both a positive and negative manner, as we all learn to ideally cooperate, balance, and harmonize with each other.

Our nightly news depicts daily examples of our negative relationships as they play out individually, locally, nationally, and internationally. The universal laws of Karma and Balance are not given equal time in our established media, which highlights only the drama of bad news, with an occasional feel-good story to end the broadcast on a more positive note.

Our world consists of many types of relationships, such as our extended family, children, co-workers, friends, and even our pets. In this instance, I wish to focus on the positive aspects and mastery of a loving, balanced, intimate adult relationship between any two people, without regard to gender, by building a sacred *relationship bridge* of mutual independence, interdependence, empowerment, and love.

Empowered interactions between two souls in a relationship ideally engage the four universal laws of Love, Light, Free Will, and Balance. Equal and balanced empowerment enhances a loving relationship, acknowledging and allowing each other the freedom of choice and free will. When you allow for true recognition of a balanced relationship, you effortlessly shift and heal old wounds and karma, create positive changes in your life, and expand your love for yourself and for others. The end result of this process is a healthy relationship.

At the soul level, we embody both the masculine and the feminine aspects. And, at the moment of our conception into matter, we choose to split into one or the other to demonstrate a feminine or masculine body throughout our physical life on earth. If our purpose is to embrace and express the characteristics of an empowered woman, for example, to assess if one can fine-tune the attributes of empowered femininity, we also need to incorporate and express our masculine traits into a state of unity. This journey at the soul level is completely understood, but, when we drop into physical form, somehow we lose this clarity.

When we are young and first dating, we remain transfixed on the superficial things such as how we look, what we wear, and wondering if he or she likes us. This represents the first stage for many of us in an adult, romantic relationship.

Accept the notion of traversing through several stages of development and growth, since it is all part of the forgetfulness of your god-self and a test to determine if you can find your way back to the androgynous wholeness of "you."

Not all adults today choose to go into a serious relationship with another. Some individuals may opt to make the journey solo this lifetime without a partner, while building a single pillar of independence, empowerment, and love rather than a bridge. The role of free choice is expressed while he or she plays out life's lessons without the interactions, reflections, and diversions of a partner. Many people prefer this purposeful direction.

I will share my personal story as a demonstration of my partnership with my husband throughout my adult life, as we joined our love together to form a "sacred relationship bridge." My story is only one in a million possibilities of what a relationship can portray.

Early on I asked myself, "How do I empower our relationship and partnership based on love, trust, wisdom, independence, and equality? How do I retain my personal power without losing it in the process of a relationship?" That is not an easy task when society dictates selected roles, rules, and expectations.

I met my husband-to-be at an early age of seventeen. He was a philosophy major at a local university and came into my life just when I was spiraling down into a spiritual hole, since I was very disillusioned with the traditional church by that time. He opened and expanded my mind to other possibilities.

He encouraged and supported my pursuit of higher education, the women's movement, and other directions of social, political, and spiritual thought. He is the love of my life since he supported my many whims, antics, adventures, and other obsessive things that had to be done "right now."

We married when I was twenty-one and had a darling daughter a few years later. She is the joy of our lives. Prior to her birth, my husband and I played, partied, traveled on our motorcycle, attended school, worked at a variety of jobs, and basically lived a simple "Hippie" life. We had loads of fun and, when our daughter was born, everything changed. I finished college shortly thereafter, and we moved to California where our "Yuppie" life began.

We joined the professional ranks of society, working and raising our daughter and aspiring to all the external necessities and niceties—the fast-paced jobs, the house, the cars, traveling, and enrolling our daughter into every activity available. Again, we had a great time, but, in the mid-1980's, I started feeling restless, stressed, overworked, and empty inside. I had all the external aspirations in life yet something was missing. Something was beginning to change in our relationship and within me.

As we grew older, I became what I teasingly call a California "Fruit Loop" and discovered the whole metaphysical world, filled with many new ideas and concepts of spirituality, while we both worked and helped each other take care of our child. By "Fruit Loop," I am referencing the beginning of my spiritual awakening to full consciousness, absent of any other religious traditions.

My husband stayed the same while I was changing very fast in a metaphysical sense. He couldn't keep up with me so we ended up in a divorce, and then I moved to the Southwest. The divorce didn't work either. After two years of separation, we got back together again and eventually remarried and continued to live in the Southwest. The point here is that we went through many stages of growth, development, disasters, and learning about the many dynamics of a committed marital relationship.

For most of these years, we changed and grew up together in a very supportive, loving, and encouraging way. However, like any relationship, we had our difficulties. It took the divorce for me to learn I could not be his mother and couldn't change him. Grasping my incorrect assumption that one can change another by smothering and mothering was a difficult lesson for me, yet a huge step forward in the evolution of our relationship.

For example, aware of my skill at multitasking, I wondered why he could not do the same. I tried to forcefully suggest (and at times coerce) him into the mold of an analytical project manager with a business plan, "to-do" lists, charts, graphs, and plotting our busy, rushed daily lives down to every minute detail. He attempted to fit the mold for a while but, as time went on, he took charge of his power and would have none of it. It took many years for me to step back and acknowledge my unconscious efforts to disempower him, and to finally allow him to choose his own way in the world, doing one thing at a time in his relaxed, calm, methodical, and logical manner.

After many years of exploring the necessary compromises of a relationship, I realized that loving our partners for who they are today, without focusing on the past or future, shapes a balanced partnership without ego, judgments, fears, doubts or mothering. Focusing on the NOW washes away the expectations, ego, drama, and the charts and graphs. Acceptance and loving allowance of another's differences brings balance, stability, and individual empowerment to a relationship. I wanted support, independence, equality, and the opportunity to discover the whole world as well as myself, yet I couldn't seem to return the gesture at first. It was a hard lesson.

With the many influences of the latest women's movement beginning in the 1960's, many conversations of inequality and even role reversals have bubbled to the surface once again. The people of our earth have a long history of preconceived superior-versus-inferior roles and expectations leading to inequality between men and women. This doctrine unfortunately projects outward between races, religions, age, and sexual orientation.

Society today seems more open to addressing inequality between the sexes more assertively. My female generation opened the door in the 1960's by rebelling against the designated roles and rules, and the younger generations (most, not all) seem to be carrying the torch further with their openness to sexual and marriage rights.

These days we all seem to be making it up as we go along, creating relationships based on equal probabilities and circumstances rather than designated roles. During this transitional time, the man as the main breadwinner and the women as the mother and nurturer have reversed in some cases or co-mingled in others, causing much confusion and stress in the male-female relationship. In my opinion, we have made progress, but we have not achieved true empowered equality as of yet. There still remains much resistance to change.

I am sure this is not new; men and women have been struggling with this for centuries. I was fortunate in that my husband allowed me to retain my personal power and encouraged me to change roles. I attended college and also took on the role as a financial contributor and breadwinner working in the corporate world. Luckily for me, women could finally climb out of the secretarial pool and pursue jobs that men traditionally held, such as sales, management, construction, news anchors, etc.

My mother was not allowed to do that. She could work but only as a secretary, nurse or sales clerk in a store. Women of her generation could never occupy a traditional male job—except during World War II, when they were allowed to work in the factories because all the men were overseas.

I am not sure where my inclination came from, but, somewhere along the line, I believed women could do more. I believed I could do more. I watched my own mother, who was very smart and capable, practically run the company where she worked. Even though she performed the tasks and accomplishments of a man, she was not considered a breadwinner for the family and was, therefore, compensated accordingly and treated as inferior, with no other job advancement or financial opportunities.

I must have sensed this injustice and discrimination and vowed I would change it. Obviously, I was not the only woman to feel this way since it grew into an entire movement.

The women changed, and men changed reluctantly. Many men supported their wives; many others did not. It was a struggle for both men and women at first. Women emerged as "supermoms," taking charge in the work world, as well as coming home at the end of the day and laboring through the housework, child care, meal preparation, and many other tasks. Many men helped with the household duties, others did not.

Again, fortunately for me, my husband took on many of the responsibilities of taking care of a home and a child. It became more of a shared job. We redefined the roles of husband-wife and mother-father. We tackled the daily duties head on without consideration of defined roles, sharing the responsibilities together.

As I step back and look at my soul's earthly purpose, I chose to participate in the corporate world to explore and anchor my masculine traits, re-uniting my masculine and feminine as one. My husband, by participating in the home life more fully, anchored his feminine self with his masculine embodiment again, rejoining as one balanced soul. We each chose to explore the illusion of duality by experiencing and shifting between female and male roles.

There are many other approaches on how to experience the separation and unification of the female/male essence. Follow the wisdom of your heart and choose the path appropriate for you.

In the United States today, things have changed even more as we strive to encourage our boys and girls to achieve their hearts' desire, whether in sports, jobs, or relationships. However, there still remain many roadblocks that hinder progress. Women still run into the glass ceiling in the corporate arena, and boys are perpetually encouraged to pursue the traditional male roles rather than, for example, the creative arts or nursing. Progress and improvements are developing yet, from my observation, our world faces many more challenges ahead.

Within the gay and lesbian community, as more and more come "out of the closet" and begin to define new roles, progress still seems hindered as we continue to judge and ridicule someone's relationship based on sexual preferences. Some cultures still forbid girls from going to school or having a job, even dictating what and where they sleep, eat or wear. The road ahead still looks like a very long one as we continue to strive for true equality for both men and women on this planet.

Women can no longer accept being treated as inferior human beings through acts of degradation, domination, humiliation and violence in any form.

Women must find a way to retain their personal power and not lose themselves in the relationship. Women must feel their inner strength and trust it. They must not sell themselves out just to fit the traditional roles. Women should rise above their negative notions and cease doubting, questioning and overanalyzing their appearance, talents, child-rearing abilities and intelligence and elicit the courage to move beyond doubts, anxieties, and fears.

Men need to learn that they, too, can nurture themselves as well as women. If men would only release their fears, unearth their gentle, feminine side, and express it more toward themselves in their relationships, they would revel in the respect, contentment, and balance it would bring them.

Both men and women need to be true to themselves and each other. This man-woman, god-goddess relationship ideally unfolds as layers and layers of confidence, equality, free will, courage, strength, love, and trust.

I like to think of the male-female relationship as a bridge that has two pillars of equal size and strength. Visualize them interconnected by a horizontal platform, with the man standing on one pillar and the woman on the other, representing their relationship. Both pillars must be of equal importance and strength or the bridge would become unstable.

If one tries to dominate the other, then he or she would show an overabundance of power and strength while the other succumbs and expresses weakness and frailty. Weakness is not an ideal situation for a bridge. A weakened section of the bridge will eventually collapse. Each pillar represents an individual with his or her own thoughts, ideas, beliefs, and values. The horizontal platform allows for loving energy and communication to flow back and forth, creating balance between the two individuals.

One should strive to be his or her own person, know who he or she is, and what he or she wants. Then one is ready to have a long-term relationship, such as a marriage, or whatever traditional or non-traditional form is preferred. Maybe you are not sure what you want out of life or what you want from a partner. I sure wasn't prepared for a long-term relationship at age seventeen. But love often seems to move people into the right place whether they are ready or not. Entering into a stable, trusting, and loving relationship can open doors for some people to discover who they really are as they lovingly and safely support each other.

This is how I see my relationship with my husband. We are two independent structures bridging our love, strength and respect for each other, and together we are empowered. We built a strong foundation of support, forming anchors or grounding cords for each other as we experienced our earthly journey. For me, he will always be my "forever rock," gently embracing and grounding me while I fly and explore the various nooks, crannies, and mountaintops of the world, while I do the same for him.

His foundation of love and support is like drawing water from a well. Charging through life with gusto and courage, my thirst is replenished and nourished as he stands beside me while we intermingle and anchor our encouragement, independence, strength, and empowerment as one. He does not stand behind me or in front or above or below but at my side, wrapped in love and equal partnership. We are each braided together in the gold and silver cords of the masculine and feminine rainbow rays of love and light. (The golden light represents the male aspect; the silver light symbolizes the female aspect.)

Probably the most important thing I have learned in this relationship is that when you tear away all the nonsense of roles, responsibilities, problems, and expectations, all that remains is love, recollecting the old Beatles song that says *"love is all you need."* It is the glue that holds that bridge together. As the years have gone by, I realize how deep yet expansive my love has become—not only for him, but also for myself.

At one point along the way, I believed it was best to relate with a man declaring very low or, better yet, no expectations at all. Most importantly, I had to learn that I can't and shouldn't even try to change him. Some would call this a bit cynical for having "low" expectations, but it was my way of pulling away all the expectations and judgments, seeing him for who he is and just loving him—that majestic male spark of a soul.

Once we transition and return to our soul-self, the male-female relationship that we have all worked so hard to understand in our external world has actually been with ourselves after all. We each hold a part of the male and female essence within us. It is simply a reflection of our need to balance those same masculine and feminine aspects that comprise our inner world. In this lifetime, I just happened to be expressing my female essence more strongly than my male essence.

The overall goal here is to balance my male and female selves. Women need to link with their masculine side and men should embrace their feminine side. It is acceptable and welcomed for men to be nurturing, soft, and even cry. It is acknowledged and authentic for women to be strong, assertive, in charge, and not cry. In the end, the right relationship is really with myself, discovering my potential within me.

My husband has been showing me how to be male, and I am showing him how to be female. Mixing up the roles has just made it more challenging, but we have both accelerated our soul journey at a much faster rate. I chose this relationship in this lifetime to experience these challenges. I emerge from it having learned the lesson of self-empowerment, understanding my feminine and masculine selves better.

Take a quiet moment to view your relationship. Perhaps you feel tired and frustrated with your job, school, children, and husband, wife or partner. Understandably, society places many pressures on relationships and families. Frequently, difficulties arise when attempting to focus on intimacy and love as life rushes around you.

We all face the many stages and challenges of development, growth and karma. See if you can shift your thoughts from focusing on the negatives and move into a place of appreciating at least one thing about your partner. Nurture that positive thought for a while and drop away all the expectations and drama. Take a few deep breaths and bring forward the love you feel in your heart. Notice that you are now beginning to create a whole list of positive attributes.

Practice this technique to transmute the negative thought into a positive loving thought. Recently, I made a list of all the things I appreciated about my husband. I gave him a copy of the list for Valentine's Day. It brought tears to his eyes. It warmed my heart, and I hold the memory dear. That simple yet profound communication instantly brought us closer together.

Search within your heart to find ways to nurture your relationship back to a place of unconditional love. The healing of our relationships in the external world begins with healing our internal world. It all starts with you and me as we shift our thoughts, words, and actions, shining our love and light outward for the good of our relationship and for the good of all. Love is the core of the relationship—the glue that intertwines your essences as one. Cherish it.

In our relationships, we choose to embody the circle of life, merging our love together to co-create and reflect our wholeness. We do not abuse our power and hold the other back or give away a part of ourselves since this creates imbalance. Together, we demonstrate the image of wholeness, the androgynous soul representing our god source choosing action or inaction. Building our relationship bridge flows in whatever proportion of interdependence and independence we choose, reminding us once again that the roadway we traverse is one of empowered expansion with the self, after all.

Our programming about love overflows with rules, regulations, traditions, fears, and expectations. I began my journey with my husband with a whole set of baggage. Yet, living with this wise man, I have released so many wounds and karma; I am now free to love openly. I am more aware, awake, and conscious of love without conditions, with more giving and receiving, appreciation and forgiveness.

As I released and cleared old karma, wounds, and energy blocks, I moved my soul closer to my ultimate goal of ascension consciousness. What an amazing feeling of joy to discover and acknowledge the meaning of unconditional love. As I give love, it instantly returns tenfold. Wow! I feel my heart soar!

I thank my husband and my whole family for teaching me this lesson. It only took thousands of miles of travel down the winding road, up the mountaintop, and around my inner world to discover who I truly am, and to shine the light on the Power of Me.

CHAPTER 18

Beloved, Be Love, Be Me

All I can do is be me, whoever that is.

– Bob Dylan

In many of my personal meditations, I frequently hear my higher self declare loudly, "Beloved, be love!" What a wonderful mantra and reminder of my true essence. However, in this earthly world of duality and separation, I ask myself about the times when I withhold love or someone withholds their love from me or I forget to *be me.*

Surrender to the ambiance of *being* the true *you* living in the present moment, appreciating and loving all of your life as a creative adventure! Make a resolution to accept the challenge to *be love* and to develop your relationships being fully conscious and present.

The even bigger point to this relationship issue is that, in my early adult years, I was so busy being a Hippie, a Yuppie, a wife, and a supermom; I was so busy *doing,* that I forgot to just *be* who I am.

In my teens, twenties, and thirties in particular, I made choices based on what others defined for me and what society expected of me. I longed for accomplishment, success, and status, always striving for more and more. I had very high expectations for myself and for my husband, and neither one of us could live up to them. Continually compelled to succeed by some external belief of what others expected of me, I lived through another's predetermined plan.

I just wanted to fit in. I went after the things that society said we should all have. Go to college, have lots of friends, earn all the money I wanted to buy things, grow up, get married, have a child, and work in a career that I loved. I wanted everything to be equal between my husband and me, and I wanted to work in a just society—all lofty and somewhat idealistic goals.

I don't regret these experiences, but I forgot one huge thing in all my efforts to fit in. I forgot about me. I forgot to live for me.

Why did I forget? I did not know myself or my deep desires and needs. My soul felt hidden from me. I did not know what I wanted or my soul's purpose in this lifetime.

Who am I really? I did not know. The demonstration of me that I expressed externally to the world at that time did not feel authentic. I understand now that my soul-self purposely veiled me in forgetfulness so I could freely experience my current lifetime at an external level, losing sight of my mission. New lessons and a new contract were waiting for me to discover my authentic internal soul-self as I chose to awaken spiritually at a later stage of my life—all in perfect order.

As I look back at my life, I reflect on the many wonderful people I have met and the adventures we shared together. In my late thirties in California, I started to meet the special people who would serve as my spiritual teachers. They opened my eyes to another way of seeing the world and myself.

My husband emerged as my most important teacher in that he taught me to think "outside the box." He helped me in my studies in college and led me to expand my thinking on a particular topic. He always allowed me the freedom to grow, to learn and to experience life.

I believe, now that I am in my sixties, I can finally give up the notion of living through other's expectations. I have been rebellious my whole life, even though I made myself try to fit in. I worked hard at it, yet I continuously fought everyone along the way, including myself.

I now know, I can just *be,* instead of always *doing.* I now understand where my rebelliousness came from. My inner voice was saying, "You don't need to fit in." I am finally living more in the present moment and appreciating it. I have found my internal peace.

This is the key: live in the present moment and appreciate it. When you do this, you come from a place in your heart, and that is a place of love. You can simply *be love.* When you are able to *be* love, you automatically bestow love freely. Share your love unconditionally, without the intruding ego mind in the way constantly analyzing and critiquing your every move.

The ego starts the conversation in my head that I should look a certain way and act a certain way, or wonder why someone does not like me. Why, why, why? I just want to scream at my mind to be quiet!

I still forget the simple act of being present and appreciating. But I just laugh when I catch myself going back to my old ways, bringing myself back to the present moment and loving and appreciating all that is in my life. I strive to look from a broader view and remind myself that the little dramas in my life are not really that important. When I observe from a larger perspective and understand it, I have discovered that this is where my power is. This *is* the Power of Me.

I love me; I accept myself; I love my life and all of my experiences. I love all the people in my life. I am not withholding love from them or myself. A few came for a fleeting moment to teach me something or for me to teach them. Many are still here with me, such as my family. With them it has been a life-long journey.

Most of my experiences evolved as positive and rewarding, yet many were not. In most cases, I was able to eventually comprehend the lessons involved.

The holographic earth school we each participate in creates an environment of continuous learning, teaching, tests and challenges. When we transition into another dimension of our self, we will continue to learn. Earth teaches us to experience duality, feel emotion, and experience the light and dark within ourselves, but in the end, we all find the light. We find unconditional love, are never alone and always guided back to the light throughout this process.

I once read that one should be "of" the world but not "in" it. In this so-called physical world of atoms that our brain sees as solid matter, it is really a world of vibrations and light. I walk this world observing and experiencing, but I am actually a spiritual being remembering my true essence--a god in training having a physical experience.

It is an illusion, after all. Our five senses have interpreted our physical world of matter as real. We live in a hologram, a pretend "game." Once I have accepted this notion, I feel I can accept myself as I am. There is *no* need to fit in; just be who I am, a loving essence and a spark of the Divine. Knowing this gives me a feeling of self-empowerment, not power over someone else, as ego would define it, but the true power within me.

Consider playing with this notion of appreciating, loving, and living in the *now*, without judgment. Watch yourself shift from negative to positive thoughts. Experience how it feels to be in the now and to feel free to be who you are.

Go sit in a public place, such as a mall, library, your workplace or wherever, and just look around. Observe all the people in your surroundings. You will make judgments. Consciously notice yourself making judgments as if standing outside of yourself. You may know some people and you like them; you feel differently about others. Some have nice clothes; others wear ugly, shabby clothes. Some are fat; others are too skinny. Some are gay; others are heterosexual. Some are bullies; others are kind. Some are happy; others are sad. You go on and on with your judgments rattling around in your head.

Notice yourself thinking these thoughts. Now try to shift them to the opposite spectrum, substituting the negative for more positive affirmations. Picture each person as a powerful, majestic being of light and equal in every way. We are all potent and very special souls coming to earth at this time to experience something unique. We are all co-creators and gods in training. Can you grasp the magnitude of this concept as it levels the playing field for all of us?

Feel yourself living in the present moment. To experience this, look around the room, for example, and observe the objects, such as the chair, the desk, the files, and the books—everything—and just feel appreciation for all of it. Feel the chair under your bottom and thank the person who invented that chair. Look at all the artwork hanging on the walls and appreciate the artists who created it. Look outside the window and gaze at the trees, the flowers, or the clouds in the sky. Feel appreciation for all of it.

Now bring your awareness back to the people in the room or area where you are sitting and see if you can feel love in your heart, honor them for who they are, and appreciate them as spiritual beings and gods in training. When you do this, you are in the present moment, looking at everything around you right now.

If you have any feelings of anger or fear, it may be hard to relax and shift yourself into this space. If so, then pick another place.

Taking a walk in nature may assist you. There you can look at a leaf and bugs, carry a rock or a stick, or hug a tree. Gaze at the sky. Just feel everything as it is right now with no thoughts or expectations.

Feel the love and appreciation of all of your observations and sensations. You are no longer withholding love from your self or from others. You are giving, receiving, and being love at this moment. Nature feels your love and gives it back to you, too, if you are open to feeling it. It may not happen today, but you will eventually experience this.

In this state of being present and being love, you will feel your internal power. Work to change your consciousness from a *thinking and doing* ego-mind and go into your heart of eternal love and just *be* it. There is nothing else to do but *be love*. If you have to *do* something, let it be an experience that creates passion and joy without busyness. Another good exercise to practice is to sit in a chair and hold your hands out in front of you, palms up, resting on your knees. Now visualize yourself projecting the feeling of love out through your hands. Try to feel the energy extending out in front of you and expanding outward.

Now reverse that. See if you can receive back the love you gave out. Feel the tingling energy pouring back into your hands and moving up into your whole body. You may not feel the tingling in your hands, at first, but practice it.

Love is about giving and receiving. By just being love, this process flows freely and effortlessly. I am not always able to hold myself in the present moment, feeling love and appreciation. I will go back and forth between periods of balance and equilibrium to being unbalanced. I will have days where I may feel frustrated, angry, or sad as I rush impatiently through my busy day. I just feel the emotions and let them play out. I eventually will move back into a place of balance, calmness and love.

Feeling emotions is not a bad thing. Emotion means "energy in motion." It is a good thing as it is part of the earth experience and part of the illusion. With the interplay of the lower ego-mind and the higher mind, I am always striving to bring myself to a higher level of consciousness and love because that is my natural place to be. Remaining in a higher vibratory state is a major challenge in this Third-Dimensional earth plane.

I had to learn to act like a two-year-old from time to time to feel my emotions. I allowed myself to fully express. After I have completed my temper tantrum, I just say, "Oh, well," I have gone through another layer of learning. I just forgive myself and know God is like a parent observing the child having a temper tantrum. Parents observe the "temper tantrum" behavior with a loving, parental eye and wait for it to pass and continue to love no matter what.

How we behave in all relationships, whether or not we accept responsibility for our behavior is an extremely important part of whom we are. How people treat each other says a lot about our culture and the world we live in today. It seems we are not doing too well overall, as many are still learning and struggling with their life lessons as they continue to search for love.

In general, we still see ourselves as separate from each other and from God, and we mistreat each other, our animals, and our earth's resources. As a world culture, we seem to accept this abuse. We observe people every day hating others because of their skin color, sexual preference, gender, age, religion, class, appearance, philosophy, or behavior.

Even someone's size gives rise to abuse, such as a big burly man abusing and bullying a smaller woman, just because he can. What we have forgotten is that if we hurt another physically, emotionally, mentally, or spiritually, we hurt ourselves. It is really our own self-esteem that is injured and, to make ourselves appear better, we belittle the other person so we can feel more important. The issue is not with the smaller woman, but with the bigger, burly man.

Strive to work on your own issues and lessons and learn spiritually correct behavior without harming another. You will discover that it will lead to more happiness and joy in your life. You will like yourself better if you make the effort to take responsibility for your actions.

Within all types of relationships, what is the proper, spiritually correct and ethical behavior, and what is the best way to *be* in the world?

Here is a list of goals or suggestions to anchor you in a place of love, appreciation, and integrity. Although obvious and easy to say, difficult to do many times, this list is definitely not complete. Feel free to add your own.

- Love yourself first before you love the other.
- Give love freely, but don't forget to receive love. It feels so good.
- Live in the present moment.
- Follow your family traditions, especially if they have deep roots. They are a part you. Honor and follow them if they resonate with you.
- Take responsibility for your behavior.
- Know there are consequences for bad behavior. Karma, or cause and effect, is at play here. If you hurt your friend or family member emotionally or physically, someday that friend will hurt you in some way in return. Remember that words can hurt too.
- Don't be a bully. Be kind.
- Be that person that knows how to be a best friend. Being there for someone at just the right time is precious.
- Respect and care about the other person, which equates to respect for self. Respect other people's belongings as if they were your own. Respect other people's time. If you are late all the time, you are implying that "my time is important; your time is not." Be respectful in all that you do. Mind your manners.
- Honor your boundaries. Respect the boundaries of others.
- Be compassionate.
- Trust yourself. Trust the other person using discernment.
- Be considerate.

- Forgive yourself first; then forgive others.
- If you have disagreements, fight *for* the relationship rather than fighting *against* it. To clarify, this means to fight to find a way to reach agreement and compromise, rather than fighting to hurt the loved one.
- Be honest. Do not lie.
- Speak the truth.
- Take a risk and express your highest truth.
- Take another risk and love unconditionally without fear of getting hurt.
- Stop hiding your true self.
- It MATTERS how you feel.
- Don't leave anything unexpressed. Don't bury your emotions and feelings.
- If you feel sad or angry, express it. Let it be. Sit in sadness or anger. It is not a bad thing. It is your truth at the moment. If you can't handle something, seek help. If you determine it is not your emotions, visualize yourself sending those feelings to the light.
- If someone you love dies, mourn him or her. Mourning is just your expression of love. The correct way to mourn is whatever works for you and for however long it takes.
- Don't hold life at arm's length. Embrace yourself and the people in your life.
- Serve others with no expectations of receiving something in return.
- Have no regrets.
- All that matters is how I RESPOND to others, no matter how others treat me.
- Understand you can't *fix* or *change* others. Allow and accept each person for who they are.
- Work together to compromise in a reciprocal manner.
- Understand your differences. Agree to disagree.
- Travel around the world to observe how other people live, appreciating their similarities and differences without judgment.
- Know we are all ONE, with no separation.
- When someone is angry with you, he or she is angry at your behavior, not the essence of you. The person still loves you. Sometimes that person is re-

ally angry with himself or herself and not really angry with you at all.

- Act in an ethical manner, not from fear of punishment or that someone is watching; do it because, in your heart, you know it is the right thing to do.
- Addictions are negative habits you use to hurt yourself. Be conscious of over-doing it with drugs, alcohol, food, sex, destructive habitual behaviors, etc. Seek help if necessary. Besides the physical damage you do to your body, addictions weaken your auric field making you susceptible to the negative emotional thoughts of others.
- Question everything, especially authority.
- Educate yourself. No one will open that book for you. Develop your curiosity and imagination. Learn how to communicate through speech and writing. Don't ignore math and science. Your age does not matter. It is never too late to learn. Start now.
- Never harm anything—other people, animals, the earth, or yourself.
- Be responsible and take care of your health. Eat right; get plenty of sleep and exercise. (A cliché, yes, as you have heard it over and over, and yet, no one will do it for you. Only you can do it.)
- Embrace change. Life has many ups and downs. It can be good and it can be a struggle. Re-analyze your goals and expectations. Don't give up. You are not going crazy. Keep striving to do better. Forgive your mistakes.
- If you are the teacher of the moment, guide your student toward self-determination, so eventually one is no longer dependent on the teacher.
- Don't take life so seriously that you forget to have fun. Laugh out loud and frequently.
- Nurture yourself.
- Nurture the right relationships.
- Nurture the right attitude.
- Nurture the right relationship with Mother Earth.

This is a very short list of dos and don'ts, but you get the idea. I could go on and on. This is all very easy to say but very difficult to achieve. The lesson for you is to find your own ethical compass, your own inner voice of knowing what to do and what is correct, and to know the difference between right and wrong—the positive and the negative, the light and the dark.

It may take you a lifetime (or two, or ten) to perfect these things. You will feel the love for yourself grow, plus you will feel the sense of accomplishment as you begin to master these skills, and your many lessons in life. Don't perceive yourself as a victim and stop trying, or give up on yourself. Trust that you have the strength and courage to know what to do, since you are a spark of God. Go ahead. Start striving now.

CHAPTER 19

The Lesson of Shadow–"How Not to Be"

What if someone gave a war and nobody came?

– Allen Ginsberg

Frequently, our lessons about duality and separation vividly dramatize our shadow self and "how not to be."

In utilizing this colloquial phrase, I am specifically referring to all the negative behaviors that people act out, such as withholding love, causing physical and emotional pain, lying, cheating, stealing, bullying, abandonment, and causing fear.

We only need to look around our planet to observe other negative actions, ranging from petty ones to the unimaginably grotesque. Yet each of us possesses the capability for positive and negative conduct. I am perplexed at, and frequently embarrassed by, how badly I can respond if I become angry or scared. I shudder at some of my behaviors.

As I look back at my life and review my bad behaviors and choices, I search within my heart to find a way to forgive others who possibly provoked me, and most importantly, to find a way to forgive myself.

I now realize that these "negatives" serve as our best teachers. It seems we have to feel extremely uncomfortable with a situation before we create forward motion. Hanging out and being surrounded by love, light, and comfort is easy. I would prefer to just sit in the light and bask in how wonderful it feels.

However, that is not why we incarnated here on this planet. We chose to walk the earth in physicality at this time to experience emotion and create our evolutionary impetus of progression. Therefore, we will have many teachers of the negative shadow enter our lives to teach us "how not to be."

Remember that duality encompasses the light and dark energies interacting with each other—the positives and the negatives. Psychic researcher and author Delores Cannon referred to the negative energies as an "evolutionary catalyst."[29] The dark and light energies stimulate our development as they interact and dance with each other. We are ***moving ourselves forward on the evolutionary scale*** as we interact with each other and ourselves. Therefore, the dark energy emerges as a catalyst.

The Dark Ones, as I call them, appear in our lives at the most appropriate moment to demonstrate the lessons of negativity. Most importantly, they show us how to shift, heal, clear, and respond better to our everyday challenges, creating movement and evolvement. Whether their acts are selfless or selfish, we are best served by giving them our forgiveness and our gratitude for the lessons. Let me explain the reasons.

First of all, the Dark Ones have chosen to play the shadow role of negativity to create movement or friction between the light and dark so we can evolve and embrace our necessary lessons on both sides. Remember, they are all sparks of God and embody love and light, yet some of them agreed to play the role of darkness for a short while.

Secondly, wrap your mind around the notion that you, too, have played this role as the negative teacher in several of your lifetimes. I find this disconcerting as I ponder the potential for me to commit evil deeds in my many past lives and my current one. Yet we witness it every day as someone acts out his or her designated role of negativity.

The idea of "how not to be" on this planet confronted and challenged me to learn the hardest and most intense lesson of all, and it has taken most of my present lifetime to fully grasp it. Once I understood this lesson and could look at my relationships from a more expansive view of duality in action, then and only then was I able to move more easily into a place of compassion and forgiveness for all the things people did or said to me that caused anguish.

Now that you understand "how not to be" and its purpose, let's apply this to our relationships. To clarify how this process works, I would like to share a very important and vulnerable lesson I learned from my father as the "Dark One," or teacher of negativity, demonstrating duality in action through the absence of love. He taught me about my shadow side and how it feels to be the recipient of negative actions in our mutually agreed upon journey and our lessons of "how not to be."

In order to understand fully the positive energy of light, one must experience the lower nature energies as well. Perhaps this is a reciprocal relationship where I withheld love from my dad in a previous lifetime and now it is my turn to experience the consequences and reverberations of such acts, thereby releasing and balancing out our karmic contract.

In this lifetime, my father set himself up to experience many negative circumstances. His mother, a strong, independent woman, shuffled him from place to place. His father, not an ideal role model, chose the path of alcoholism, beating my dad with a whip and performing other cruel deeds, creating a very difficult childhood.

At age eighteen, my dad enlisted in the Army and fought in World War II. Toward the end of the war, in December 1944, he was captured during the Battle of the Bulge in Belgium. He only wore overshoes (no shoes or socks), and they forced him to march with frozen feet for two days into Germany where he spent his time in several different prison camps. He just barely survived the ordeal and dropped to 106 pounds and became quite ill, emotionally and physically, when finally released in April 1945. This entire traumatic situation, in addition to watching his friends die of starvation, spearheaded a major turning point in his life. It changed him.

My dad recovered physically, for the most part, except for some old injuries and stomach problems, but he never recovered emotionally. He has lived his entire adult life with post-traumatic stress disorder (PTSD). According to the National Alliance on Mental Illness in Michigan, "PTSD is an anxiety disorder that can occur after someone experiences a traumatic event that caused intense fear, helplessness, or horror."**

Shortly after the war, he met my mother and they married and had three kids—two girls and one boy. I am the oldest. I remember my dad telling us kids to never come up to him or touch him while he was sleeping. Because of the PTSD, he was always afraid he would wake up screaming and swinging his arms around in utter terror and hurt us. He said if we needed to wake him, we could only wiggle his feet.

Also, in later years, if he ever started talking about his experiences with the war, he would break down into tears. I grew up with all this pain and fear and with this war in my dad's mind. Being the empath that I am, I felt all of his pain and torment as I described in a previous chapter.

His war became embedded in my mind. I never enlisted in the Armed Services. I did not need to, since I had already fought in a war at a deep level and knew what it felt like. I never understood any of this as a child—or why my dad behaved the way he did. After all those traumatic experiences, my dad became a very mean alcoholic. His personality turned from a nice dad into a mean one in an instant—a very fearful, vulnerable, and unstable situation.

Now, as an adult, with a more spiritually mature understanding, I accept him as my most important teacher of "how not to be" and without judgment. This revelation was a huge step forward for me. Many books exist about "children of alcoholics" and how it affects their lives, so search them out if you need further understanding. All I ever wanted was a "normal" dad. To me, as a child, he was unable to give me his love. He never learned it from his family and losing all his friends in the war just shut him down completely.

I know deep in my heart he felt love; he just didn't know how to express

---

** For further information, go to www.namimi.org and do a search for PTSD.

it. I love my dad, but as a child I found it confusing and hurtful that he could not return that love. Instead, he completely shut down and remained emotionally unavailable and non-supportive to me. Barely able to hold himself together emotionally, "being there" for us kids became a crushing burden for him.

The hardest part occurred when he drank and his personality would shift in an instant, numbing himself and burying his own emotions and demons in the alcohol. Unfortunately, alcoholics do not comprehend what they do to their loved ones, as we each learn to cope with and enable his bad behaviors.

The harsh lesson of emotional and physical abuse, ridicule, and withholding love deeply wounded me with no real outlet for my pain and need for genuine communication. My dad was incapable of expressing his feelings.

I have heard the term "Silent Generation" in reference to World War II vets. They just "buck up," bury their emotions, and "act like a man." That description fits my dad. Luckily, the Armed Services are beginning to understand more about PTSD and how to treat it.

Instead of talking and discussing things in a calm, rational manner, my family responded by yelling at each other in anger, trying to find ways to hurt one another by saying and doing cruel things. Not the best way to behave; yet it became each of our coping mechanisms. I continuously struggled to fit in with this family that taught me "how not to be."

As an adult, I educated myself about PTSD and alcoholism. The family even tried "alcoholism intervention" to no avail. Dad refused treatment, which was extremely traumatic for me.

How do you reach someone who refuses to get well? I learned the hard way you can never change other people when they refuse to take responsibility for their actions or non-actions. But the journey helped me to understand what happened to him and why he drank and, most importantly, what lessons we jointly agreed to teach each other in this lifetime.

I still have very deep wounds from the experience. I continue to relive it, feel it, cry about it, and work to release it. When I step back and review my life, I am overwhelmed by the lessons we learned together.

My dad and I chose to share this lifetime together. From a spiritual perspective, he accepted this assignment to be born experiencing the negativity of war, lack of love, loneliness, and alcoholism. What a huge revelation it was, when I discovered his purpose in demonstrating his negative shadow-self to me, his daughter, and how not to act in life. In order for me to muster the strength to find love for myself, he showed me how not to communicate, how not to behave, and how not to love. He demonstrated these things to me so I could feel the emotion of hurt and pain behind these acts.

My lesson in this lifetime immersed me in the negative side of emotion, and what better way to safely experience it than with a significant family member such as my father. My mother and siblings, also acting as teachers, agreed to participate in this illusion of the shadow self. Experiencing the many gut-wrenching negatives of emotion within the circle of duality did not feel good at all.

As a child and even for most of my adulthood, I could never understand him and why he behaved this way.

As I look back into the early years of my marriage, I became starkly cognizant of my inability to demonstrate love to my husband, and I shudder at the pain I caused him. Luckily, he loved me so much that he just kept showing me his love until I finally surrendered my resistance and habit of withholding love. I opened and released my heart from its hardened walls and loved him in return expansively. I could finally release my self-preservation coping tendencies and finally give and receive love unconditionally.

It took many years of practice. What an amazing sensation within my heart and soul once the floodgates of love gushed open.

I do catch myself from time to time, "holding life at arm's length," as Dr. James Martin Peebles frequently says. But I feel love well up in my heart now and I can express it. The love is so intense that I sometimes cry just because I can't contain it. My dad taught me all of this and my husband too. They both enlightened me on how to give love and to receive love.

The negativity of not loving creates the friction of movement forward so we can return to a place of love, which is where God is—our true home. My dad and I had to take this journey together in order to find love again. I forgive my dad and I forgive myself. Forgiveness combined with appreciation creates the awareness, allowance, and release of the pain and trauma.

I have moments when I still forget this. A visit back home quickly re-ignites those old wounds of pain and confusion, recalling the alcoholic's behaviors, and I revert back to my old patterns of anger in which I frequently lose control of my emotions. He behaves badly and I react badly. I feel the old wounds surfacing again.

I finally granted myself permission to limit my visits back home as I fell deeper and deeper into the old flashbacks of pain. I decided to change the way I participate and move to a place of detachment and neutrality. I incorporated many of the skills taught in this book to attain this aspiration.

I recently came to the abrupt awareness that I too suffer from post-traumatic stress disorder and could no longer expose myself to those old patterns of pain and flashbacks. It certainly explains my incessant busyness to hide from my pain or my strict, unbalanced guarding, boundaries, and protections designed to avoid some of the negative emotions and disruptive surroundings.

One of the last visits triggered the old, dark muck at the bottom of my psyche exposing my deep cellular/emotional memories of abuse. As they exploded to the surface and into my conscious mind, they revealed the deep pain I was hiding within myself.

This explosion of emotion actually burst open my cellular memory blocks and released my painful deep-seated recollections once and for all. They were no longer hidden but out in the open, very raw and ready for me to release and heal. Sometimes we have to hit bottom before a complete release and healing can occur.

I explored many gut-wrenching emotions as all this came to light. Living with the illusion of "pretend" that my family's interactions functioned on, it became completely unacceptable for me. I acutely recognized that nothing would change, and holding out hope that someday Dad would acknowledge me for who I truly am was fruitless and would never happen. He was incapable of communication and recognition of his own attributes and limitations, or those of other family members.

I made the difficult decision to mentally and emotionally break ties with my family, with one exception. I went back home to help with the final stages of my parents' life, as they moved into assisted living and we put their home up for sale.

For some of you, making a complete detachment from a toxic family or other situation is necessary to heal and one should allow for this separation without guilt, as appropriate. At first, the loss evoked a grieving process, yet, symbolically, it became necessary to fully heal and release my expectations, pain and trauma.

At some point, I believe we must all take our power back, detach and release the old patterns to make room for the new, whether it is a loved one, a situation or purpose that no longer serves us in a healthy, productive manner. I grappled with the struggle between the old, wounded self and the new—the one living in the present moment, looking from a new perspective.

What is that perspective? What story do I choose to live that will set me free? What will be my mindset? Do I choose anger, bitterness, harshness, or pain? Will I surrender to the opposite virtues without expectations, and shift to compassion, love, forgiveness, detachment, and mercy?

From my recent visit, I confess I have only attained the first stage of healing which is awareness and acknowledgment of the fresh, reopened wounds. It may take me a while to reach the next stages and return to my place of balance, love, and forgiveness, but I will eventually ground my core essence within my god-center as I remember my power to choose love.

In all my NOW moments, this has been my test of self-mastery, self-empowerment, self-love, and joy as I bless all my actions, non-actions, and interactions, fully expressing gratitude and appreciation. I allow this mantra to flourish in my mind, opening the many doors of my psyche granting permission for my wounds to finally heal, as I release all expectations.

The moral of the lesson revealed that I am actually withholding love from myself. Why do I mistreat myself? When I figure out why I am withholding love and why I am not treating my inner child better, I will solve the puzzle. I will re-evaluate my perspective and look through my god-eye as I come to the realization I am no longer the child victim, but a god in training mastering the skills of detachment, free will, and empowerment.

I have learned enough from my father; now I must go within, honor my inner child, my divine destiny and wake up to my own empowerment by beginning to love myself even more, as I strive to be my own best friend. I am sure my healing process will continue to unfold and evolve as I go deeper into the discovery of love and lack of love for self—the next lesson.

I share all of this with you so that you can learn and benefit from my own journey. I believe that when we remember our stories from the past, we heal them. Sometimes we all need a little nudge and reminder. That's when I turn to my great friend and teacher, James, who patiently and lovingly guides me back to my true self. Thank you, James.

Thank you, Dad, for making this huge sacrifice in your lifetime of negativity to teach me how to find love, compassion, empathy, and how "not to be." And thank you, Ed, my husband, for supporting me throughout this whole ordeal. All of you contributed to my process of healing this in myself. And thank you "self" as you took me to the depths of my shadow and brought me back again safely to the light.

I needed to experience the dark side of myself, heal it, and find the light again within me. For this huge lesson, I express my deepest gratitude. I have heard it said that to truly understand and appreciate the light, one must also experience the dark. This whole experience emerged as a huge test for me in this lifetime. I know deep in my heart that I have passed this test and am now ready to move on to the next set of life's lessons. This is something we all need to do to reclaim the Power of Me.

I often wonder if this universal law of balance, the karmic circle of light and dark, cause and effect—is *purposeful*. Are these concepts of positive and negative attributes God's creations or man's experiments with light and dark? No one knows for sure.

I contemplate why a loving God would create negativity. I suspect this ***is*** purposeful and part of the grand blueprint of creation. Perhaps God intended the laws of the cosmic universe to act like the gentle nudging of a parent guiding a child to understand the ways of the earthly world, with love and trust in the wisdom of the child. My soul knows why I chose to experience light and dark, as I search within for my definitive answers to the mystery of myself and of God.

You too, will undergo many negative experiences in your life. We all agreed to the concept of duality when we incarnated here. It is not easy, but find a way to transmute the negative into a positive. Forgive yourself and then the teacher who taught you this very hard lesson of "how not to be."

I challenge you to speculate on the mystery of your shadow. Examine your life and search for your karmic lessons. Recognize that as you release resistance and "stuckness," you take a giant step forward into your own personal graduation to enlightenment and empowerment.

PART TWO

The Great Awakening

CHAPTER 20

Graduation/Ascension and the Great Awakening

When the power of love overcomes the love of power, the world will know peace.

– Jimi Hendrix

We are living in one of the most exciting eras on Planet Earth! Many ask how that can be true with all the discord and chaos we see all around us in the world. I propose we each take a step back from our everyday activities, look at the bigger picture, kindle our imaginations, and shift our perspectives with a welcoming, open mind.

In the remaining chapters, I will outline one possible reason to explain why we are living in a most glorious time and how the coming shift in consciousness will change the world. Other people propose several scenarios with grains of truth. Again, I encourage activating a healthy dose of discernment in whatever stories come upon our paths of awareness. No matter our perspective or interpretation, we each feel a stirring in our hearts and souls that something BIG is about to change!

Many believe that the entire cosmos is about to launch into a mass ascension as we all shift into our next level of learning. This is not only a rare event, but also a beautiful and exciting time to be alive in a physical body experiencing the breath of life.

Each of us is part of the collective consciousness moving toward a universal mass spiritual graduation or, more accurately, an ascension, which moves us to a higher level of vibration and learning. Specifically, we are collectively moving from the Third Dimension to the Fifth Dimension and beyond.

Perhaps that is why we have seven billion people on earth right now in physical bodies. We all want an opportunity to experience our personal graduation and ascension from matter on the earth plane, as well as the grand spiritual ascension for the collective.

This will happen simultaneously on all planets, solar systems, galaxies, universes, omniverses, dimensions, and parallels. It is a very special time and many ancient prophecies speak of this event. Some said it was the end of the Mayan Calendar that occurred on December 21, 2012, or the end of life as we know it. Most of us see it as a new Golden Age* rather than a doom–and-gloom scenario.

Whatever name you call it, the goal here is for as many of us as possible to wake up spiritually, to move to the higher vibrations of light, and ascend without fear. This is what is referred to as the "Great Awakening" or the "Great Shift to Full Consciousness."

This means that our bodies would become less dense, vibrating at a higher frequency and shifting from physical to physical-etheric beings. Our cells will be crystalline rather than carbon-based, and dwell between both worlds of physical matter and light, luminous bodies. Our DNA will have multiple strands, not just one double helix. The positive and negative energies will be transmuted, transformed, and transcended into balance. We will all have more clarity of the soul-self, and many of our gifts of telepathy, healing, teleportation, etc., will be restored. We will no longer need to release the old karma, since it will all be cleared.

Will this all happen suddenly in one day? I doubt it. According to our perceptions in the third dimension, the process unfolds slowly even though it may only be a blink of an eye in a cosmic sense.

From now on and into the future, this Great Awakening unfolds as an evolvement in individual and mass consciousness. Therefore, begin to visualize our third-dimensional earth releasing and clearing the old energies, fears, and karma bringing in the new energies of unconditional love, which allows the vibratory rate to increase, thereby making it easier for the awakening process to take place, with less effort and resistance.

Perhaps, you will eventually notice negativity starting to decrease in the world. Maybe you will gradually see more people working together in community, rather than alone and in a competitive, combative fashion. Begin to witness the washing away of hardship and fear as we go through this process, with no destructive end of the world—simply ***a shift in consciousness.***

Take notice of these improvements and favorable changes. Some will endure difficult transitional periods before things sort themselves out, but they will all move in a positive direction of love, harmony, and community. We will learn to empower others and ourselves through the use of inspiring words, thoughts, actions, loving support, and encouragement. By focusing on our positive thoughts and deeds, we easily ground, integrate, and master the universal laws of Love, Light, Free Will, and Balance realizing our full potential.

If we choose not to graduate and/or ascend this time, either consciously or unconsciously, we will have many other opportunities to do so. Again, the goal for each of us in this particular lifetime is to come to the classroom of earth, learn our lessons, pass the test, graduate to a higher vibratory level of learning, and join the Grand Ascension, if we so choose.

Similar to elementary school, you move up to the next grade level as you accomplish your reading, writing, and math skills. Eventually, you receive a degree that says you have achieved a certain level of expertise. At the soul level, free will and free choice always plays a significant role in the personal graduation process. Love and recognize your inner core strength and power while making the choice to take charge of your life.

Now is the time for all of us to choose to awaken, advancing in our own way and time, physically, emotionally, mentally, and spiritually according our missions. A personal graduation from matter transpires as a very individual, gradual process and not in a one-size-fits-all way. Our personal goal is to wake up to our true soul-self, move to the light, and ascend to a higher vibratory rate. You declare your intent to be part of this grand ascension, choosing to follow your heart and soul, always in alignment with love, light, free will and balance. Take the high road in all you do, as explained throughout the chapters in this book. Learn to be present, living in the *now,* staying alert and consciously observe what is happening around you.

The balanced or neutral point between good and evil, light and dark, is choice. What behavior, thought, word or deed do you choose? As you stand at the head of your path, what preferences do you embrace?

Strive to reach the neutral point of balance by acting impartial and detached to everything around you. Your individual graduation involves releasing all old karmic wounds and the ego-mind transcending to the universal mind. Begin incorporating into your life the many spiritual practices, such as good conduct, maintaining a healthy body, mindful living, conscious breathing, meditating, serving others and understanding the power of your oneness. Begin to focus on your inner realm, while also enjoying the outer world.

For you, perhaps, it can be a mysterious journey not ever fully understanding your purpose or mission in this lifetime, yet, you continue to pursue the search for your personal graduation on faith and love alone, no matter your religion, non-religion or level of spiritual development. Whatever path you endeavor to follow and are drawn to, you can actualize all your choices, desires, and dreams, if you faithfully trust the process, knowing all is in right order.

We never stop learning, no matter what planet or plane of existence we may reside on. We all step into the next level of learning that all souls want to manifest. There are many levels of graduation from matter and many levels of spiritual ascension; you choose which one you will experience. There is no judgment, no failing grade, no after-school detention—only free will and free choice to experience your soul's adventures at your own pace.

I know I am ready to graduate and unite with the Grand Ascension into the Golden Age of love, harmony and peace. I am excited to see what my soul has in store for me, next. I sure hope I can spend a little time on the "Vacation Planet" for a while, before I start the next set of lessons and co-creations. This earth school has been a tough one. I need a Spring Break. Let's all party.

CHAPTER 21

The Test

The mind is everything. What you think... you become.

– BUDDHA

How do we graduate and ascend from our earthly Third-Dimensional plane of existence? We pass the many tests put before us. They are our life lessons. We designed the exam before we incarnated here in our physical body.

Envision a grand academy on our planet where we are taught and tested on the many challenges of duality, the light and dark vibrations of the universe. Somewhere along the line, our souls decided that we needed to learn to pull the two polarities of light and dark, positive and the negative, together to neutralize it, to expand our growth and ultimately balance ourselves. As we change and grow, so does everyone else in the many universes.

It is important to realize that as you work to change and balance your vibration, you bring all of creation along with you, because we are all interconnected as one. There is a payoff to all of your hard work, as you search for the meaning and values in your life. As you benefit, we all benefit.

On many planes of existence, souls live in continual light and love. Perhaps everybody, including you, confronted the deep desire to expand universal wisdom, along with relieving a little boredom while in the spiritual realms, and decided to accept the opportunity to experience life in the world of matter. It is a possibility....

Nonetheless, at some point, you decided to expand your knowledge by delving into matter. What better way, than to be born onto the Planet Earth classroom and immerse yourself in the lower, denser energies?

As mentioned earlier, we forget our true soul-self at birth, so we could enter the journey called "physical life" to eventually remember whom we are, which is our eternal source or the universal mind.

The test is to see if we will remember our soul-self even though we have put the obstacles of forgetfulness, blindness, and struggle in our way.

We experience the lower energies such as pain, fear, prejudice, hatred, judgment, anger, guilt, cruelty, etc.; the list is a long one. However, we also have many things on earth that remind us of our light, too. On the external level, Nature, her symbols and cycles have many things to teach us about love, light, and balance. Master Avatars,* such as Jesus, were born on this earth to demonstrate love and compassion. He did that through his actions and his words, showing us that the true Christ is a vibration of love.

Our many relationships also teach us about love. The test then is to find our way through the darkness of our internal ego and mental mind of negativity and return to our positive universal mind of light, our true soul-self.

To pass the test, we all have many opportunities, choices, and lessons on how we evolve in this lifetime experience. There are a few other concepts we need to incorporate into passing the test, besides finding love, forgiveness, appreciation, etc. We also need to move beyond beliefs to knowingness, move our mental mind to the universal mind, pay attention to our thoughts and learn to act or react in a positive manner rather than a negative manner, and to connect and listen to our inner soul voice.

This is a huge task. However, by starting here, you truly do build your foundation to find the key to your soul and return to your true home of light, love, and balance, the womb of the Creator. Understanding the difference between a belief and true knowing is crucial to finding the key to your soul and passing the test.

To believe, according to Webster's Dictionary, is "to have a firm conviction about something; accept it as true, or to hold as opinion." Believing is also used in the context of a "religious conviction." If you think about what "belief" really means, the key word here is "firm conviction."

The foundation of a belief is, therefore, a system that controls and limits you to the world of illusion. It entraps you. I do know, for myself, that this is where the religions of the world limited my thinking, by moving me inside the box of what others believe—their "firm convictions."

All religions contain many truths. However, what is truth for you may not be my truth, and vice versa. Beliefs may serve you for a while and be a place for you to start. But it is very important that you learn to eventually connect and listen to your own soul voice—your intuitive "knowing" voice.

Shift yourself to a "knowing" state of mind. Nothing can change or influence you when you know. Change your words from "I believe" to "I know." Above the celestial "tabernacles," it reads, "Know thyself." You must learn to trust your knowingness.

KNOW means:

K Know thyself and be determined to overcome

N Negativity

O Opening the divine circle of illumination, the circle of oneness

W Using wisdom[30]

In addition, the word "know" integrates the word "now." *I "NOW" it to be. I proclaim it to be.* As reiterated before, practice changing your vocabulary of words to vocalizing the positive, rather than the negative, limiting expressions. Know that you always have free will and free choice to pass the test and move to graduation or you can choose to *bypass* the test in this lifetime and address it in another. You have a choice of what words you use.

Another very important key to passing the test is to learn to move from your mental mind into your universal mind.

As infants, we learn to explore our Third-Dimensional world with such enthusiasm and awe at the physicality of everything. Our brain sees everything as solid, dense objects. We experience all of life's nooks and crannies. We discover our five senses. We touch; smell; see; hear and taste. Such fun! We are beginning to discover our mental mind as defined by our physical brain. We discover emotion; all of it, even loving and enjoying the extremes of those temper tantrums.

Coming from the etheric realm and entering this dense, physical world is a shock and drastic change. Many of us still remember our etheric world and our soul-self as an infant, but in time we forget. We buy into the limitations and illusions that density creates.

The ego plays a part, as well. It was actually created to be our defender, rationalizing and guiding us through life; that other little whisper in our head that says "Don't do that; don't touch that… Turn right; not left…." The ego rationalizes, makes excuses and defends its positions.

Ego justifies the illusion and creates camouflage to cover up our true reality of soul-self. As time goes on and we grow older, we start to learn the rules and customs of our family and our society, in general.

For many of us, we initially forget who we are, stay spiritually asleep to our *true soul-selves* and let our ego take over our mental mind. We forget we are spiritual beings having a physical experience, not the other way around. The ego mind depicts self-centeredness, exclaiming "it is always all about me." Frequently, we also allow the ego-mind to violate our power and boundaries, by allowing someone else to tell us what to do.

As children, we are told what to do all the time. Learning the rules and the customs of our society and culture functions as our main assignment during childhood. Generally, it is acceptable and expected to be spiritually asleep during this time. (Some of the children remain asleep; many of them are wide-awake.) As we get older and move into adulthood, we need to wake up spiritually and move from our mental/ego-mind and find our own knowingness and our soul voice, which is connected to the universal mind.

Moving into your universal mind, guides you to your life's purpose and your passion. You know what you love and what to do. You don't doubt yourself any longer. You just know. Trust that mind and acknowledge it. You may not understand your life purpose at this time, but eventually, as your life unfolds, you will discover your purpose—your passion.

Your universal mind will guide you to your purpose, if you listen for it. Your purpose can be something as simple as showing a smile to the clerk in the retail store, or you may become a world leader. Whatever it is, there is no status or valuation of your purpose. All purposes are equal in God's eyes.

How you love and what you magnify to others shines the light of "you." Be open and willing to share your many gifts. All anyone wants is for you to be your authentic self. Your wealth, your clothes, your gender, and your looks, do not matter. ***Your achievements in passing the test are measured by how well you have acted, how well you reacted, how you thought, how you loved, and how much you gave to others.***

If you think about it, this is all you have to *do* and *be* on this planetary school called Earth.

This leads to the next part of the test, which is to pay attention to your thoughts and know the difference between the positive and negative ones. Learn to act and react in a positive and loving way. Don't let negative thoughts and behaviors become a habit.

Now is the time to conquer your chattering mind. Trust that you have the power to change your thoughts. If you are spiritually asleep—and not consciously aware of your universal mind—and only caught in your ego-mind, you will not be aware of the difference between the two.

As mentioned earlier, thinking a certain way all the time will become a habit. If you constantly feel anger, your first response is to react in anger. Instead, think of another way to respond and shift your thinking to a positive approach. Rather than blowing up at someone, try to understand where the miscommunication comes from and see the other person's point of view. Practice this. It is not easy at first, because it is a habit, but give it a try.

Another common behavior is that we often have negative talk going on in our own heads. Affirmations and positive expressions or thoughts help us to shift our thinking.

For example, if stuck in a negative thought such as greed, search for the opposite, which is generosity. Simply make a list of your negative thoughts and convert them to positives and then vow to take action expressing those positive thoughts and words. It is that easy, yet we make it difficult by forming habits of negativity. When we accentuate the prominent positive thoughts and release the negative ones, we instantly manifest new outcomes. We are that powerful.

In Louise Hay's book, *You Can Heal Your Life*[31], the author professes that a person's negative thoughts can lead to a physical or emotional illness. She compiled a great list of illnesses or emotional upsets and describes the problems, their causes, and a new thought pattern to replace them.

For example, Hay claims that if you have general back problems, the back represents the support of life. You can affirm to yourself, "I know that life always supports me." If you have specific lower back problems, the cause is "fear of money and lack of financial support." The new thought pattern for that ailment is to say to yourself, "I trust the process of life. All I need is always taken care of. I am safe."[32]

Connecting and listening to your soul voice is another section of the test. When you connect, listen, and know your truth, nothing else matters; you can transcend whatever is there. Let yourself feel the joy. Listen to your inner soul voice. It will show you the way. If you require guidance and assistance, seek help from your guides and teachers. All one needs to do is ask.

Jesus listened to his inner soul, his universal mind. He recognized the difference between light and dark, which allowed him to know what to do.

For example, when he was fasting for forty days and forty nights as the story goes, Jesus was tempted by the dark energy. "And the devil said unto him, if thou be the Son of God, command this stone that it be made bread. And Jesus answered him, saying, it is written, that man shall not live by bread alone, but by every word of God." [Luke 4:1-13.]

The ego-mind was trying to control him. The lower nature wanted him to fail. Jesus recognized this negative thought coming into his head and said that he knew what he was doing. "I am going about my Father's business," he declared. He stayed focused on the light, his positive thoughts, and his intentions. He had passed this particular test by holding true to his connection to his universal mind and listening to his purpose and his truth. This was his demonstration of how to make the choice to move from the negative thought to the positive one.

The time is now to make the decision to find the keys to your soul. Build your foundation of truth and inner knowingness. Your soul knows what to do; it will show you the way. You just have to quiet yourself, ask, and listen for that soft, inner God-voice that is your divine knowing, wisdom, and light.

You will get an answer. You will feel the joy and peace that comes with your inner knowing. You will be guided to pass the test; let God know you are ready to join the Great Awakening.

CHAPTER 22

The Ancient Souls Return: Clearing the Old to Bring in the New

Grandfather, look at our brokenness. We know that in all creation... only the human family has strayed from the Sacred Way. We know that we are the ones... who divided... and we are the ones... who must come back together... to walk in the Sacred Way. Grandfather... Sacred One... Teach us love, compassion, honor... that we may heal the earth... and heal each other.

– Ojibwe prayer

The American Indian Elders declare: "we are the ones we have been waiting for!"

Deep in our souls we intuitively know how to touch our collective hearts, uplift and heal our human spirit and our beautiful earth. The time for that profound and magnificent event is now.

At this pivotal point in our universal history of mass ascension, the ancient souls are returning to facilitate Mother Earth and all of her inhabitants in the ascension to the Fifth Dimension of creation and beyond to release and transcend old karma. You and I are those *ancient souls.*

As mentioned in earlier chapters, the earth exists in perceived duality and separation. This means that it inhabits an environment comprised of both light and dark vibrations. The light vibrations dwell within a higher love frequency and are closer to the God source. The dark vibrations resonate at a lower, denser frequency, and are further from the God source. Yet, an aspect of God abides in both.

Within the total darkness always hides a spark of light. Darkness or shadow enhances beauty and should not to be feared, but, merely represents an absence of light balancing the two polarities into neutrality.

We, as the ancient souls and co-creators of Atlantis, Lemuria and other realms, have chosen to reincarnate on earth once more to release old karma and to further experience duality this time around, so we can evolve and remember we are gods and move beyond the illusion of separation. We need to experience our shadow side in addition to our enlightened side neutralizing the two polarities.

Thousands of years ago, the ancients fully expressed love and completely embodied the light—the original intent of this planet. The ancient civilizations collectively shared a clearer connection and an open consciousness with God and the cosmos, embodying a more "spiritually awake" persona with intact talents and gifts such as telepathy, teleportation, healing, etc. We can see remnants of these civilizations today in their ruins scattered around the planet.

For example, consider the Egyptian and Mayan temples and pyramids, or the Celtic stones such as those found at Stonehenge in Britain. No one today can carve stones and place them on top of each other with such precision as these ancient cultures did. We continually explore their technology, presenting many theories, yet we discover it can't be replicated.

One current theory involving a Sumerian Tablet, called the "seated giant," proposes that sound frequency and magnetic energy were used to transport heavy, carved stones into place. What an amazing concept that is, by today's standards. The wisdom of these powerfully, advanced technologies still reside within us; we just need to remember how to do it. And it all starts with you.

The time is *now*, especially since the younger children being born today carry the DNA structure to support this wisdom. Their predecessors, the Light Workers,* have laid the groundwork for these spiritually gifted newborns, joining us on Earth at this time. These children offer hope for a magnificent, new future.

Now, more about the past.... Ancient civilizations left behind many monuments of wisdom, and records of their achievements contributing to our spiritual evolution. Look at each continent or island on this planet, all depicting myths and stories of the fascinating, productive ancient traditions and systems.

For example, many have studied the ancient ways of the American Indian, the East Indian, the Asian cultures, the Aborigines, Celts and other European cultures, the Minoans on Crete, the Middle Eastern cultures, the South American cultures, the Eskimos, the South Pacific cultures, and the African cultures. Each one demonstrated fascinating ways of interacting with Self, each other, nature, Mother Earth, the stars, and their God source. All the ancient cultures expressed the same message of love, light, law, free will, balance, and truth. Each of these civilizations devised different names for their creator. They looked to the stars, because they knew that was their home.

Imagine the billions of civilizations among the stars, planets, solar systems, galaxies, universes, omni-universes, dimensions, and parallels. The Earth exists as one of many, within this grand cosmos. (Suggested reading for further understanding: *Worlds beyond Death* for multi-dimensional information).[33]

Right now, as of this writing, we have no official proof that life exists on other planets, but it is just a matter of time before our world governments are forced to reveal the truth of extraterrestrial life. Too many of us have seen the ships and the lights in the skies. The ancients believed we came from the stars to inhabit this planet. As noted earlier, they arrived with all their wisdom and gifts intact. Then one day, that all changed.

Here is one interpretation about what happened. Some people may see this story played out differently. That does not mean they are incorrect; it merely reflects their experience or understanding, as just one piece of the many significant variations in existence. This may be your first introduction to some of these concepts. Absorb what you can, and please explore other sources of information, as you search for clarity. This is my memory of the stories, as told by Orpheus Phylos, Angela DeBry, and Alijandra.[34]

A galactic war* was raging throughout our universe. (*Star Wars* movies probably offer a fairly accurate description of the horrific turmoil.) A race of physical-etheric beings who split from Oneness challenged the status quo, creating unrest on many planets by fabricating negative thoughts. One day, they set their sights and destructive intent on a planet in our solar system called Maldek.

These negative physical-etheric beings eventually took control of the Maldekian people and no longer allowed freedom of choice. Destruction, misuse of power, negative cloning, greed, monitoring of thoughts, installing implants, and so on, caused a great decline in the beautiful, harmonic culture that once prevailed.

Some of the warm-hearted Maldekians resisted and left the planet. A few came to earth to build a new, harmonious life, along with many other planetary civilizations, to colonize and create what is known as our ancient Lemurian culture. Eventually, with the misuse of atomic energy (the fire crystals), the negative physical-etheric beings blew up the planet Maldek and destroyed it completely. Remnants of this planet's debris are found in our asteroid belt.

Here on Earth, as the centuries went by, some of the Lemurians wanted to break off from the Lemurian continent to establish a new colony. Falling prey to negative thinking and losing their connection to Source, this group began using fear and control as their objective and rejected the harmonious culture of love and balance. Just like some on Maldek, a few negative thinkers broke away from Lemuria and established their own colony called Atlantis. These Atlanteans wanted to take control of the planet and chose to abuse their power by becoming greedy and abusive, so they began "negative cloning" and using the "fire crystals" or nuclear power energy.

Eventually, just like Maldek, the Atlanteans abused their power to the point of causing changes in the electromagnetic fields and vibratory levels of earth, causing much upheaval and huge earthquakes. This event brought about the complete destruction of the main civilizations called Atlantis and Lemuria, which caused complete shifts in the positions and shapes of all the landmasses, plus the emergence of new mountain ranges and oceans. It also caused the loss of xenon and other gases vital to our life force. This started the change in our DNA, which caused us to lose our many gifts of telepathy, understanding of our Oneness, etc.

The remaining Lemurians and some Atlanteans who did not agree with the negative thinking began migrating all across the earth, creating "schools and storehouses of knowledge." These are still located in our pyramids and many other hidden vortexes on the planet. Some of the Atlanteans with the negative thoughts also survived, reincarnated and are still working with the intent to control and to keep us in duality, fear, and separation to this day.

Since this destruction on Maldek and on earth, we and our space brothers and sisters have been working for eons to restore our abilities and to balance Mother Earth and all her inhabitants—human, animal, plant, mineral, everything. Since that happened, we have all been stuck on the "Wheel of Life," a karmic circle of light and dark, with the dark representing control and fear. This control takes many forms including mind control.

If you look around, fear and control still exist today. We are repeating the same karmic, negative patterns we started on Maldek, Lemuria and Atlantis.

It is all about to change and you are part of that process. Our space brothers and sisters (extraterrestrials/ETs) have worked to restore the xenon and other gases on the planet. They have worked to keep the nuclear weapons in check, and they have joined with us under the guidance of the God source to assist us in making the shift back to our true selves as beings of light.

However, keep in mind that the ETs will not directly save us as dictated by the galactic laws of Free Will and Free Choice and the non-intervention clause. They cannot interfere with our preferences, but they may guide us. *We* are the ones we have been waiting for to correct the misdeeds and miscreations on our planet by collectively acting responsibly and lovingly for the good of all. The decision is ours to make and, with divine assistance, we can turn our despair and frustration into hope and action for the betterment of mankind and the restoration of our planet.

Were all of the galactic wars and the destruction of Maldek and Earth's Lemurian and Atlantean civilizations necessary or planned? I am not sure, but what if they were created and planned to detain humanity and other celestial beings into a place of darkness to experience duality for a time?

In the end, to understand light, we must acknowledge and experience our dark side. What if we, as co-creators of God, planned this so we could understand our shadow side? God, acting like a loving parent, would sit back and watch as his children created, explored, and experimented with light and dark.

Maybe our experiment went bad. We became entrapped and stuck on the karmic wheel and now our celestial friends, who are no longer stuck, have come to our aid. I also believe many of our ET friends have chosen to incarnate (be born within a physical body), on Earth so they can experience duality, and to also serve as a liaison with the higher realms. Right now Earth is the only planet in this universe that represents duality.

Perhaps you are one of those ETs choosing to go through the birth process to experience earth and facilitate the upcoming changes. Earth is not your home planet, but you chose to be born here to experience duality, release old karma and heal our planet this time around. (Those from the celestial realms are called the Star Seeds and Star Children.* Those souls who reincarnated on earth only are called Star Lights.*)[35]

Right now the earth is evolving into higher dimensions of light. The changes are rapidly happening now. And this is where you, and especially the children, come in. The children being born now have a different DNA structure and are evolving back to the original DNA intent of love and light.

Mother Earth, in all her love and support for us, dropped her vibration down to a lower level so we could all play with duality for a while. Earth is now increasing her vibratory rate and changing her cellular structural level, going back to her original intent of love and light without duality. This is why the earth changes are occurring.

The ancient cultures predicted this time of change. Some called it a time of graduation or ascension and others called it Armageddon or the end of the world and the end of time. The world is not ending. Mother Earth is changing and evolving to a place of light.

The ones of the dark side who still want to use fear to control us will call it end times, the end of the world, or Armageddon. It is not happening that way. We are moving into higher dimensions of being—from the Third, then to the Fourth, and now into the Fifth Dimension. As we move into the higher vibrations, our wisdom and our gifts are being restored.

This is actually a very exciting time to be in the physical body. From a spiritual standpoint, being in a physical body accelerates our spiritual soul's growth at a much faster rate. We evolve much quicker that way. Lowering the vibratory rate into physicality promotes rapid expansion of wisdom and maturity, adding a rare expertise to our Akashic Record or soul archives.

That must be why the earth is so overpopulated right now. Some ETs (Star Seeds and Star Children) have chosen to incarnate on earth right now. Not only did we want to experience duality, but we also wanted to experience ascension—the shift back to the original intent of light, love, law, free will, balance, and truth. We all want to ascend together.

Therefore, there is no need to go into fear, as we see changes going on in each other and on Planet Earth. All is in divine order and playing out exactly as planned. Perhaps this is the grand plan, after all, and not an accident in co-creation or an experiment gone badly. It is the mystery of God. We will not know for sure, at least for now.

At some point in my evolution, I plan to ask God to explain the whole thing. Perhaps when I die and transition to another place, my full wisdom and power as a co-creator will be restored to me and I won't need to ask; I will already know. Sometimes, in my moments of frustration, I think this duality system amassed a few flaws and I plan to discuss them with the appropriate galactic federations, or God. Whoever is in charge… this experiment needs a few refinements. Perhaps, after we complete this mass ascension, all the refinements will be complete.

Let's move into the present time on earth. If we look at our current history, in the last few thousand years, we continue to see good and bad: many wars, famines, marvelous inventions, innovative technologies, and improvements in education and health care. But we still have a long way to go.

In the 1960's, the children of that time were beginning to feel the "shift"—the new "love" vibration coming into the earth, and they called it the "Age of Aquarius." Unfortunately, we saw the love turn into fear, hate, and destruction as the children rioted and demanded change, but were beaten, harassed, and jailed because the older generation and the political systems feared the changes.

Starting in the late 1980's, the vibratory rate was changing and becoming less dense. People could feel the energy, heal, channel, and manifest change in their lives much more easily. It initiated a process to clear all of the bodies (physical/cellular, emotional, mental, and spiritual), and transpired in such a way so that it would be slow and gradual. If activated too quickly, the whole planet and the universe could implode on itself.

So, with divine guidance, a clearing process began on August 17, 1987. Many people were opening up to their psychic gifts, and could feel and see with their sixth sense that the vibratory rates and clearing processes of each body were changing. They called this movement the "Harmonic Convergence."

This started a cycle of "clearings" of the old ways and gradually began to open us up to many of our true gifts. The original wisdom and inner empowerment was flowing to us faster and clearer than ever before.

In the past, the monks who spent hours meditating in their monasteries on the mountaintop could tap into this wisdom, but with great difficulty. The vibratory energy manifested so densely, that a monastery life was the best strategy to connect with the sacred knowledge.

The chart below highlights the time line for this clearing process of each body, starting in August 1987 with the Harmonic Convergence. This process repeats and continues beyond 2022, as outlined in the chart below, until we complete the shift in consciousness and manifest the mass ascension. Each cycle magnifies and intensifies the clearing, healing and balancing of the energies as indicated, reaching its peak in 2015, and begins to slow down as we enter Cycle Five.

According to Angela DeBry in an article in the *UCM Quarterly* and Alijandra in her book entitled *Healing with the Rainbow Rays, The Art of Color*

Energy Therapy,[36] the following chart shows specific dates of each body being impacted during the year by an intense outward flow of energy to facilitate the clearing process.

DeBry states:

The cycles represent the energy to clear, heal and balance the four bodies: physical/cellular, emotional, mental and spiritual. This clearing encompasses karma, cellular memory, ancestral memory and spiritual alignment just to touch a few. It really is person-specific according to our mission statements for coming to Earth.

During these cycles, all four bodies experience many symptoms as we maneuver through them. For example, in the Physical/Cellular clearing sequence, we can experience heightened physical ailments or even unexplained illnesses. In the Emotional and Mental sequence, our capacity for emotional outbreaks increases or, perhaps, we are struggling with mental tasks such as forgetfulness. Whatever the challenge, remember to allow for these occurrences to work through our systems as we become more aware, release, and heal our old wounds and issues with focused intention.

Suggestion: Seek medical advice if you are not sure of your symptoms. Oftentimes, bodywork such as massage, chiropractic, physical therapy or acupuncture, etc., can facilitate your physical healing process. A soothing hot bath with one cup of Epsom salts is beneficial for relaxing the body and clearing the auric field. Perhaps a counselor may be helpful if your emotional issues become too much to handle by yourself. Experiment with what works for you to manage your symptoms.

As I look back at my own clearing cycles, I can recall experiencing a period of time with intense physical complaints. I reviewed the chart and realized that was my time to clear out my old physical/cellular memories.

The process certainly does not flow easily; it can be extremely painful and challenging. If I am unable to complete the clearing during the first cycle, the same issues will reappear in the next cycle. I am so (reluctantly) thrilled to have another clearing opportunity to finally release and balance the persistent issues.

Taking a look back at specific timeframes, I finally understand the importance of my experiences as I transformed, transmuted, and transcended myself back to a place of clarity and balance. I utilized the many tools explained in this book to recover from such episodes, particularly the grounding, clearing, balancing, and protection techniques. Each of us must labor through these cycles and there are no shortcuts.

As I have mentioned before, when you clear your baggage, the collective clears, including our Mother Earth. Review your life and the dates below and reflect on how you have participated in this process.

I have included five cycles beginning in 1987, but more may be needed to achieve mass ascension. Each cycle begins on August 17 and continues for seven months until March 17 of the following year. The spiritual cycle lasts for three years, and within the second portion, we complete it with six weeks of intense energy outflows from each of the thirteen rays of creation. Please note, for brevity, this second portion is not included in Cycles 1, 2 and 3.

Cycle 1

	Begins August 17	*Ends March 17*
Physical body	1987	1988
Cellular body	1988	1989
Emotional body	1989	1990
Mental body	1990	1991
Spiritual body	1991	1994

Cycle 2

(For the second cycle, the energy is magnified by 100,000.)

Physical body	1994	1995
Cellular body	1995	1996
Emotional body	1996	1997
Mental body	1997	1998
Spiritual body	1998	2001

Cycle 3

(For the third cycle, the energy then squares itself. The reference of "square" means *the product of a number multiplied by itself.* For example, multiply 100,000 times two and the product is 200,000. Take the product of 200,000 times itself and it equals 40,000,000,000. This represents a huge increase in energy magnification very quickly from cycle two to cycle three and four.)

Physical body	2001	2002
Cellular body	2002	2003
Emotional body	2003	2004
Mental body	2004	2005
Spiritual body	2005	2008

Cycle 4

(For the fourth cycle, the energy squares once again.)

Physical body	2008	2009
Cellular body	2009	2010
Emotional body	2010	2011
Mental body	2011	2012
Spiritual body	2012	2015

In Cycle 4, during the second portion of the fourth spiritual cycle, we complete it with six weeks of energy from each of the thirteen rays of creation. For example:

Red Ray	08/17/13 - 09/28/13	Physical Grounding Energy
Orange Ray	09/28/13 - 11/09/13	Physical Creative Energy
Yellow Ray	11/09/13 - 12/21/13	Physical Power Energy
Green Ray	12/21/13 - 02/01/14	Physical Healing Energy
Rose Ray	02/01/14 - 03/15/14	Emotional Healing Energy
Translucent Blue Ray	03/15/14 - 04/26/14	Emotional Communication Energy

Indigo Ray	04/26/14 - 06/07/14	Mental Psychic/Logical Energy
Violet Ray	06/07/14 - 07/19/14	Mental/Spiritual Energy
Silver Ray	07/19/14 - 08/30/14	Spiritual Feminine Energy
Gold Ray	08/30/14 - 10/11/14	Spiritual Masculine Energy
Clear Ray	10/11/14 - 11/22/14	Spiritual Clarity Energy
White Ray	11/22/14 - 01/03/15	Spiritual Protective Energy
Black Ray	01/03/15 - 02/14/15	Spiritual Movement Energy

Cycle 5

(For the fifth cycle, the energy begins to slow down and only doubles in vibration and intensity from this point forward. It is not known at this time, how many more cycles are needed to complete the clearing process before mass ascension is achieved.)

	Begins August 17	*Ends March 17*
Physical body	2015	2016
Cellular body	2016	2017
Emotional body	2017	2018
Mental body	2018	2019
Spiritual body	2019	2022

During the second portion of the fifth spiritual cycle, we complete it with six weeks of energy from each of the thirteen rays of creation. For example:

Red Ray	08/17/20 - 09/28/20	Physical Grounding Energy
Orange Ray	09/28/20 - 11/09//20	Physical Creative Energy
Yellow Ray	11/09/20 - 12/21/20	Physical Power Energy
Green Ray	12/21/20 - 02/01/21	Physical Healing Energy
Rose Ray	02/01/21 - 03/15/21	Emotional Healing Energy
Translucent Blue Ray	03/15/21 - 04/26/21	Emotional Communication Energy
Indigo Ray	04/26/21 - 06/07/21	Mental Psychic/Logical Energy

Violet Ray	06/07/21 - 07/19/21	Mental/Spiritual Energy
Silver Ray	07/19/21 – 08/30/21	Spiritual Feminine Energy
Gold Ray	08/30/21 - 10/11/21	Spiritual Masculine Energy
Clear Ray	10/11/21- 11/22/21	Spiritual Clarity Energy
White Ray	11/22/21- 01/03/22	Spiritual Protective Energy
Black Ray	01/03/22 - 02/14/22	Spiritual Movement Energy

From this time line, each of the bodies—the physical, cellular, emotional, mental, and spiritual— were given an opportunity to clear out the old karma and bring in the new blueprint of love, light, free will, and balance. As the current populations have cleared and healed the old wounds and karma of Maldek, Lemuria, Atlantis, and more, our bodies have moved into a higher vibration.

The purpose for the clearing cycles is to release the density of matter and shift our bodies and consciousness to crystalline light energy, achieving our ultimate goal of mass ascension. As we maneuver through these cycles, the positive light intensifies along with the dark energies.

Therefore, for a time, it may seem like the dark forces are dominating the world, as we are frequently dismayed with our negative nightly news or our personal experiences. In actuality, the dark is accelerating too. It manifests as an acute friction to create intense change and movement—and what a roller coaster ride it can be. Eventually, we will reach balance and neutrality between the two polarities, creating our vision of Heaven on Earth.

Those of us who started this process are called the "Light Workers." We awakened sooner to our true selves, so we could teach others about the coming changes. We started the preparations for the new earth and for the new children being born.

Some members of the "Hippie Generation" are comprised of the ancient souls, also referred to as the "Star Seeds." They are reincarnating from other celestial realms to give birth to the new DNA children, and to teach them to re-establish the old wisdom of the star colonies of light. Some people have referred to them as the "Indigo Children"*[37] who will, in turn, give birth to the "Crystal Children."*[38]

That could be you—the Millenials* and beyond! You are what have been termed the "Crystalline Children, Star Lights, Star Children and angels on Earth."[39] You are the transitional kids who will continue and may even finish the process of bringing yourselves and Mother Earth to ascension; the shift back to your original intent of life, love, light, free will, balance, law, and truth, with no veils of forgetfulness of your true soul-selves.

Your parents and your grandparents will be right alongside you, experiencing this clearing process. However, it will be harder for some of the elderly who still carry the old wiring. Many souls may not choose to join this enlightening journey at this time. We need to love them and accept their choice.

Many older folks do not understand the new technologies coming in. That is why your grandma or great-grandma can't understand the computer or the cell phone or the ATM machine. You probably understood all of that at the age of three. You are much more gifted and technologically evolved already, just by being born during this time of transition.

You need to understand that it has been very challenging for those who went through the earlier clearing process to muddle around in the thick density of the old earth energies, so they may be a little slower than you. I ask that, with this understanding, you graciously show patience with the older ones. After all, they willingly traversed the path through the clearing process to pave the way for you to be born into a lighter vibratory rate.

As we each clear and heal ourselves, we also clear and heal the planet with our thoughts. Our thoughts are that profound. They multiply and eventually expand to facilitate full consciousness. One idea or thought can expand, influence, and change the world. (For a better understanding of how this works, see the Appendix for the "100th Monkey Concept.")

Therefore, for older Light Workers, it was their mission and purpose to open the doors of change for their children. At some deep unconscious level, they knew what they had to do. They love the new children. You bring them joy. You are all worth it. They did it for you, for themselves, and for God.

Who are you—the Crystalline Children? You already know. I am sure neither I, nor anyone else, need to tell you. You know you are special and different.

We are currently in a transitional time as of this writing, so the older Light

Workers want to make sure you don't get off track, pushed aside or not listened to, as we each experience and integrate these changes. In twenty years, after you have gone through the current and much outdated school system, college system, or corporate world, you will see what needs to be upgraded, enhanced and/or deleted. Change it! Do it!

As you grow older, you will become more conscious of the earth and her natural cycles, so you will innately know not to hurt her and respect her biological rhythms. You will find many like-minded people and you will flourish together. Your careers will be more "green," as we currently say, and you will strive to incorporate more environmentally sound policies to facilitate healing and balance for our beloved Mother Earth.

Study the old Native American or other indigenous philosophies from around the world if you like, but I am guessing you will already know and understand their profound teachings of oneness, harmony, love, and self-empowerment. The indigenous peoples of the earth are the original keepers of Mother Earth's knowledge. They just were not listened to, and in many cases, almost destroyed in the process.

We appreciate the wisdom keepers and thank you and love you for enduring the many centuries of hardship. The awakened adults and children will now listen to you and honor your wisdom and power. We now join together as the visionaries and masters, the ancient souls returning, to heal and clear the old wounds of our past, and welcome the dawn of new beginnings of Heaven on Earth.

Allow it to sink deep within your soul, acknowledging we are the ones we have been waiting for. We represent the "second coming of the Christ Consciousness." Our global mission is to wake up spiritually, graduate, and ascend with love, peace, and joy along with the arrival of the magnificent event of ascension of the cosmos. We must embolden our intent, knowing that one thought, one idea, and one person can change the world.

The above scenario is one vision of historical and future possibilities. Many more will be revealed. Allow for the many scenarios to unfold without fear, judgment or resistance. Will you join me in this vision of uplifting the human spirit and our beautiful Mother Earth? She is beckoning us to fulfill our destiny.

CHAPTER 23

Mother Earth Is Calling You!

When it is dark, you can see the stars.

– Persian Proverb

This brings me to the present moment here on earth as a planetary being. The earth right now is very sick. She keeps holding on to keep everything safe, but that will all change in the near future. The indigenous tribes have spoken for eons about these earth changes.

We are very fortunate to live on earth at this time because the planet will graduate to another level of consciousness. We have a choice right now to uplift and ascend with her or not. If we shift with her, we need to hold our love in our hearts, keeping our thoughts and actions positive as we release all forms of negativity. This will open our hearts and minds to the vibration of Oneness finding the light within.

The dark will no longer be able to exist on earth because the planet will be vibrating at a different level of light, where dark cannot survive. Those who choose to continue to work from the dark levels will not be able to function on earth any longer. Remember, if we choose to transition, we will continue our spiritual journey of learning somewhere else. There is nothing to fear.

If we choose to stay on earth, we will all be amazed at how even more beautiful the planet will become as our earth radiates love, light, harmony, and joy, while hate, fear, crime or survival issues wash away. We will maintain our physical bodies, as we evolve into physical-etheric beings (moving from a carbon-based body to a silicon-based, crystalline form), using the full potential of our mind's capacity, not just a small portion of it as we are now.

As our senses become more acute and more spiritually mature, we feel and see the vibrations of the earth more clearly. We will remember who we are, shedding the veils of forgetfulness. We will all work together to rebuild Mother Earth to restore her to the majestic being she really is and stop destroying her. Nature is not here to serve humans alone, or to be destroyed and depleted of all her resources. Instead, we are meant to live with her in a symbiotic relationship, loving and appreciating her beauty.

As the earth's reconstruction nears completion, the probability exists that we will experience a few days of darkness. If this occurs, I gently suggest you focus on keeping yourself grounded, balanced and free of fear. When the sun reappears, the earth will be a place of beauty. Please trust that everything will be in divine order.

Some sources say that the celestial beings from the stars will come to help us rebuild Mother Earth. Again, it is very important that you do not fear them. Use your discernment. You will feel their love, knowing they are here to help, and not destroy or control us. Welcome them with your loving heart. When this happens, earth will become part of the galactic federation of star nations.[40]

You now have some knowledge of what is happening. As we create our new world, the possibilities are endless. As we focus our intentions on the probability of Heaven on earth, it will manifest as such. Probability lines of prophecy change as our thoughts change.

The choice is ours to make. We stand at a crossroads. As we create our new world, what would you choose among the infinite possibilities? Do you continue on the road of duality, or do you choose to ascend with Mother Earth to another level of consciousness? Wake up to who you are. There is no incorrect choice; there is no wrong answer. Walk down the path of your truth and choose what resonates with you.

Magnify your *Self.* Magnify your *Love.* Get out there and demonstrate to the world who you *are.* Don't hold back. Express and experience your life with passion. Step into every minute of your day and change the world, holding the love in your heart firm and knowing the power of you. You are part of the collective thought of love because we are all *ONE.* Do you remember the lyrics of John Lennon's song "Imagine"? *Imagine if all the people lived as one.* He knew… It is coming. The time is now!

With knowledge and experience comes understanding.
With knowledge comes power.
Wake up and choose.
We are the ones we have been waiting for.
The time is now!
Be love!

– The American Indian Elders

CHAPTER 24

If I Only Knew...

If you want to know your past,
then look at your present for it's the outcome.

If you want to know your future,
look too at your present for it is the cause.

– BUDDHA

I am taking a risk in these pages sharing with you my very personal and, at times, gut-wrenching experiences, interpretations of religion, politics, proper behaviors, ethics, and even the extraterrestrial question. My whole objective has been to provoke your own thoughts and to elevate them toward a more expansive view of yourself, others, and the cosmos.

I am sure there were many instances where you disagreed with me. I hope so, since that revealed more clearly your own personal truth—sharpening your discernment, knowingness, boundaries, and empowerment.

By looking at the world and all of our interactions with each other from a broader perspective, it is my hope that it helps you deal with the mundane dramas with more ease and grace. As a result, you won't allow yourself to be drawn into the theatrics of life as deeply.

The first step in our spiritual journey begins when we ask: "How do I flip the switch on the searchlight of my mind and access my internal compass that will show me the way to a better understanding of my life and purpose?"

Perhaps you have already begun your journey and are wondering what that next step is. Contemplating some of the basic principles and premises underlying this book may help you to progress more rapidly. Sometimes it takes a review of your life to see what is not working. I encourage you to broaden your perspective and expand your consciousness as you search for answers to improve yourself and your world.

Writing this book was one of my life's aspirations and it is part of my contract in this lifetime. For me, another side benefit for writing this book is that it has helped me transform my pain into a learning tool for others. The writing process has enabled me to go within, contemplate and internalize my life's journey at an extremely deep level. As I wrote, I healed myself turning this whole process into a wonderful benefit for me and I hope for you.

In the past I was so busy running around taking care of all the external things of life, that I forgot to listen to my own internal voice. Writing has helped me take the leap from a chaotic, outer world into my serene, internal one—and what an extraordinary world it is—where the true Power of Me resides.

My wish for you is that you experience all the external beauty and challenges the earth offers, but please do not forget to go within and explore your inner world. I spent most of my life shutting out that inner world and it has taken years to open the door and return to that powerful place. It didn't seem like anyone else was experiencing all these surreal visions, feelings, and voices. I kept thinking I was losing my mind or that I was delusional, so I just kept it inside and hid it from everyone including myself.

Exposing all the information, insights, theories, and possibilities of my adventures was very difficult at times, since I had been shut down in my current life and in many of my past lives, (banned from the village, burned at the stake, etc.) In my early stages of awakening, my body would begin to painfully shiver and shake, as if in shock, as I spoke my spiritual truth. I concealed all of these strange experiences, hiding them deep within myself, so I could fit in with everyone else. If I only knew at that time how traumatically I had lost my way.

I realize now that I obscured my authenticity. With this book, my truth and authenticity bursts forth, as I take the risk and finally allow my voice to flow without the constraints of current or past-life fears. This is a new beginning for me, to move to the next level of learning; I forgive myself for those old beliefs and fears, and the guilt and shame that held me back. I forgive my ancestors and others, who held the mirrors of reflection that taught the lessons of love and lack of love.

I am fully awake now, knowing whom I am and what I represent—a star seed acknowledging my power of unconditional love.

I encourage you to learn from my experiences and enjoy your external earth journey as well as your inner one with openness, tolerance, patience, happiness, acceptance, and peace. Bring balance into your life. Have fun, laugh, and take risks, experience relationships, nature, parties, sports, knowledge, and all of the external adventures. Take care of your body, eat healthy, and be kind to yourself and others. Be courageous and compassionate. Serve others.

Remember to bring your inner journey to the forefront and enjoy it as well. It is your path back home to the Great One within—the internal voyage of surrendering, transformation, integration, and awakening.

Another benefit I have just realized, is that when I write these words, God is using my mind and my hands to create this book. I am bringing God's thoughts out of the ethers and grounding them into physical manifestation. My experience becomes God's experience and that fills both of us with joy. Profound, is it not?

As I have said, writing this book has been an amazing experience. I have worked on it for about seven years now and I am amazed at how all of these words flowed from my mind and soul. Many of these ideas have been from several, wonderful teachers who have come into my life, either in person or through a book, or my own personal experiences. The kernels of truth you each shared have inspired me to think about them, feel them, discern them, and come to my own conclusions about my personal journey.

In my seven years of writing and editing, I have found that I have grown tremendously, as described above. In the editing process, I also found I had to change some of my words or ideas, because I realized I was incorrect in my perspective. I had evolved enough to recognize that some of my concepts were not accurate. They were no longer my truth. I outgrew them. I had learned to view them from a higher perspective—another way of seeing, hearing, touching, tasting, and smelling life in the Third-Dimensional reality.

Since we never stop learning, I may reread this book in the future and find more things to change or expand upon. You will just have to read the next edition or my website to learn more about my discoveries of my god-self. Perhaps I will write a book for children.

I also know that my perceptions and concepts barely scratch the surface of creation. My search for understanding the mysteries and reaching for the stars will continue. This is just the beginning....

Thank you for sharing my personal journey to self-empowerment. I hope it has helped you to expand your thinking about what is really going on in this classroom called Planet Earth. I hope it has helped you to trust your inner-knowingness. Remember to be love. You are a spark of God.

God bless you, indeed, my dear friends, as you enjoy the journey to your own heart and certainly to your own enlightenment; simply lighten up just a little bit more. Share your inner light with the world through your hands, through your ears, through your heart, through your mouth. And my dear friends bring this light to the world and you will never ever have to ask for forgiveness again. God bless you, indeed.[41]

– Dr. Peebles

APPENDICES

It Is All about Our Children

Parents often think that they are here to guide the little ones. When – in reality – the little ones come forth with clarity to guide you.

–Abraham

This section is written for today's parents. You have a very spiritually gifted child with the new DNA, and you may not be sure what to do or say sometimes or how to handle him or her. (From now on, I will refer to your children as "them," even though I am referring to your individual girl or boy child.)

Many thoughts, visions, and ideas are coming to your children at a rapid rate. Even at birth, there is a very vivid memory of their past lives and they can see into the future even though they cannot convey any of this information to you verbally. It is their experience, nonetheless.

In early childhood, the youngsters may have extrasensory experiences. You just need to know it is happening, and do not fear it—accept it. The most important thing you can do is to avoid talking them out of it. Do not discount it and say, "Oh, that is just your imagination," or "That is not true." It may not be true according to the five senses, but it is true from the sixth sense.

Just encourage them to believe in themselves and in their own truth. If you discourage, belittle or stifle their inner world adventures, you can possibly close them off from their gifts for their whole life. It can be difficult to open up that door once it has been slammed shut.

Their truth may not be your truth. Perhaps, you can use some of the concepts in this book to teach and empower your children to love and trust who they are. Just use your common sense in guiding them, and *trust* yourself, too.

Encourage your offspring to explore the inner workings of their mind. It is healthy to do this and you will raise children who will have developed a trust for their own inner wisdom.

You have this trust, too. However, most of us older adults were never really exposed to such wisdom when we were growing up. It just wasn't talked about that much. It was simply shoved under the rug, feared, ignored, or shunned. People are often afraid of the unknown.

The children today already have this understanding. In many ways, they are more advanced than we are. Therefore, we must nurture this wisdom, allowing it to flow forth and become part of their world. Be comfortable with that. We all have our own path and our own lessons to learn in this lifetime. You have your lessons; your youngsters have theirs. When you allow this wisdom to come forth, you teach your children to trust, to have tolerance for other viewpoints, to know self-love and truth.

If you think you are not very good at this, remember that perhaps your children have come into your life to teach you this lesson. Enjoy the journey together. You will be amazed by their wisdom, if only you will listen with an open mind.

Some children may be slow at learning to talk. That is because they remember what it is like to be telepathic in other spiritual realms where speech was not necessary. Don't fear it or be concerned. Just know it and work with your children. They will eventually learn the ways of the earth as it is now. (Please seek medical advice if you are unsure. Trust your own intuition.)

Remember that your children chose you to be their mom and dad in this lifetime. If they were born with physical or emotional problems, know that these special children selected you because they knew you could help them through it and that you could handle it (even though you may not always think you are handling it well). You were chosen because of your abilities, understanding and love.

Everything is in divine order and is playing out according to the master plan that was set up before you and your children were even born. Acknowledge that you are the parent and the teacher; yet, consider that your children's role may be to teach you a variety of lessons in this lifetime. Role reversals are common, so strive to be willing and open to them.

I recall and chuckle at the many times when I encountered a power struggle with my daughter. I often questioned who was the parent and who was the child in a particular circumstance. She frequently reversed roles and acted like the parent or teacher. I had to pull myself together and re-evaluate the situation and say, "Hey, I am the parent/teacher at the moment." In those instances, she attempted to become the parent. Perhaps, she was my mother in the last lifetime and she remembers that relationship.

When I accepted the teacher-student dynamic, the interplay between us flowed more smoothly, allowing the role reversals to take shape, fostering her growth and independence, and knowing I was always the parent who made the final decisions. This is not always easy with an intelligent, energetic, and strong-willed child, yet fostering that was exactly my intention as she matured into an adult.

The world will be a different place in fifty years—all because of the gifts of our new generation of children. Enjoy the ride and the journey without fear. Follow the children. They know the way… Trust in yourself because you know the way, as well. You may have just forgotten while you are here on earth.

You are in the awakening process too. God has not forgotten you. You will be reminded, in case you have forgotten. The children will remind us. For further clarity, remember to reread the chapter on empathy to understand their awakening and empathic sensitivities and to read other books, such as "The Indigo Children" [referenced in Footnote 37] and the "Children of Now" [referenced in Footnote 38]. Search out other informative authors, such as Doreen

Virtue "Indigo Evolution," or Maureen Healy, "The Energetic Keys to Indigo Kids." Many books on the topic are available.

Nurturing and respecting the power within you and your children will heal and uplift your human spirits, as you each discover your own truth, inspiration, joy, and peace. Love your children as majestic sparks of God. Enjoy your journeys of self-empowerment together!

Remember the Children

BY DIANNE HODGES

Remember the children for they remember us.
Look into their eyes of light; you can see all their love and trust.
They remember who they are and what they're here to do.
Our veiled eyes have forgotten them even when they say, "I love you."
They act out, shoot each other, get drugged or depressed,
Because we don't recognize them for whom they are, as the God and Goddess.
They're born with a new consciousness—with a vision of a new day.
But we label them, we test them, we drug them; they scream back at us
and say, "NO WAY!"
"Watch us and learn, as we are rebellious to your old ways.
We know how the world should work," they say,
"So please join us as we begin a new day."
Today is a new day for me as I look over this land.
The new children have arrived, remembering I AM THAT I AM!

Oh, yes, now we remember you.
We welcome you.
We love you.

The Hundredth Monkey Phenomenon: The Power of Collective Thought

Kodoish, Kodoish, Kodoish, Adonai Tsebayoth!

This phrase "ties together all biorhythms of the body with the spiritual rhythms of the over-self body, so that all circulatory systems operate with one cosmic heart beat.... They use this code to connect their mind with the Mind of the Father, which allows them to rejoice in the Wisdom transplanted into the mind of creation." [42]

– J.J. Hurtak

Author Ken Keyes, Jr., states in his book that the Hundredth Monkey Phenomenon "shows that when enough of us are aware of something, all of us become aware of it."[43]

In the 1950's, scientists observed one 18-month-old monkey on Koshima Island in Japan washing the sand off of her sweet potato. She discovered that it tasted much better without sand all over it.

She taught this trick to her mother and then to other mothers. More and more adults imitated their children and also washed the sand off their sweet potatoes. Over the years, more and more monkeys in the tribe began washing sand off, as well.

The theory concludes: If you have ninety-nine monkeys that learn this technique and consciously show and teach others how to do it, then suddenly one day, unconsciously, this technique can miraculously appear miles away on the next island. How can this happen?

The scientists theorized that, by adding the hundredth monkey to the equation, they communicated this technique telepathically.[44]

Thus, according to Keyes, "When a certain critical number achieves an awareness, this new awareness may be communicated from mind to mind. Although the exact number may vary, the 'hundredth monkey phenomenon' means that when only a limited number of people know of a new way, it remains the consciousness property of these people. But there is a point at which if only one more person tunes-in to a new awareness, a field is strengthened so that this awareness reaches almost everyone."[45]

The point here is that you may be the hundredth monkey to change the world or the thought patterns of the world. We are all important. We are all needed to connect our power with our spirituality and focus our thoughts in a positive, loving direction. By anchoring ourselves in the vision of peace, joy, abundance, unconditional love, and light for all on our beloved earth, we do indeed create our own reality.

ARE YOU THE HUNDREDTH MONKEY?

The Solar Cross Song: The Power of Collective Love and Healing

"Magic is believing in yourself, if you can do that, you can make anything happen."

– Johann Wolfgang von Goethe

"All I Ever Ask of You Is to Remember Me Loving You"

In 1989, a group of seekers from the organization called "Solar Cross, A New Beginning" traveled to the Yucatan Peninsula for the purpose of shifting trapped energies, releasing and healing old souls, as well as connecting with the old Lemurian time vaults (the non-physical depositories of ancient history of lost cultures such as Atlantis, Lemuria and Sumeria). In one of our healing ceremonies at the edge of an ancient, huge, deep well, we chanted the song, "*All I ever ask of you is to remember me loving you*," repeating the mantra thirteen times as we danced in a circle. When we completed our ceremony, our Mayan guide gleefully noticed that the birds once again returned to fly and swoop over the well and dip down for a drink. He said they had not flown over the area for eons of time ever since the well was used for human sacrifice. As we cleared the negative energy, the wise birds returned, offering us confirmation of the power of our collective thoughts and love, activating our higher minds to heal the area, as well as the exponential impact on all of humanity. Looking back at that magical moment, I reflect on the true, collective power of love, and the realization that when we clear and heal one, we clear and heal all of us.

GLOSSARY

Akashic Records – A cosmic spiritual library or an "energetic imprint" of your soul's thoughts, words, deeds and actions since its inception and first incarnation. They represent your private, personal records of all your lives. You review your records after each lifetime to see what you have assimilated and integrated; then you set up a new contract with yourself, laying out the lessons you plan to learn in your next life. The aggregate of these records for the many represents the data of all creation with a direct link to the God/Source.

Alijandra – During my studies and travels with Angela DeBry of Solar Cross in the mid-to-late 1980's, I met Alijandra, a renowned color healer and teacher. As a healer myself (although I did not know it at the time), I was drawn to Alijandra and her teachings of color energy therapy. I was fascinated with the concepts of the healing process by facilitating and empowering the 13 Rainbow Rays of Creation for others and myself. I explored the many facets of the healing process, learning how to ground, clear, balance, protect my energy field, and the responsibilities and boundaries involved with being a healer.

Ascension – a major shift in consciousness. Ascensions occur continuously and simultaneously at the personal, planetary, galactic, universal, and omni-universe levels moving from one dimension to the other. Some also refer to it as a graduation.

Avatars – ascended masters of Light residing on multiple planes of existence.

Summer Bacon – Trance Channel for Dr. James Martin Peebles. Synchronicity was working very well for me when I met Summer Bacon in Sedona, Arizona, in 2002. She is a trance channel and channels profound principles and teachings from Dr. James Martin Peebles, who lived on earth during most of the 1800's and died in 1922. He traveled the world healing and ministering to the people.

When he died, (transitioned) he became enlightened and chose to continue his work through trance channels such as Summer Bacon. Summer resides in Sedona and offers Dr. Peebles' channelings through classes, lectures, and individual readings. Summer has also written a book entitled *This School called Planet Earth*, filled with Dr. Peebles' teachings.

Summer, as a spiritual seeker, agreed to allow the spirit of Dr. Peebles to speak through her vocal cords to communicate messages that are appropriate and for the highest good of the listener–a process known as trance channeling. To trance channel means to translate the message of spirit by allowing spirit to enter into your physical body and borrow your brain and sometimes your vocal cords for a while. It is a cooperative effort between the spiritual entity and the channel. There is no possession, only agreement and a surrendering to her process as a trance channel for Dr. Peebles. Think of it as talking with the angels. As Dr. Peebles says, "It is a joy and a blessing when man and Spirit join together in search of the greater truths and awareness."**

The main principles that Dr. Peebles' professes are: "Number One, have loving allowance for all things to be in their own time and place, starting with yourself. Number Two, increase communication with all of life with respect. Number Three, take self-responsibility for your life as a creative adventure for through your choices and perceptions you do indeed create your reality."**

These principles are recited at the beginning of every lecture or class and it is also at the beginning of Summer Bacon's book. While easily said, it may be difficult to incorporate into one's life.

I attended many of Summer's lectures and classes and deeply absorbed these principles and more into my being. Dr. Peebles discussed many concepts such as love, compassion, appreciation, healing pain, healing relationships, surrender, trust, discernment, the illusion of separation, and other concepts of Spirit. Over the years, Dr. Peebles used many examples to explain and expand these principles so people could incorporate them into their life in a practical way.

Many of these teachings expanded my perspective more fully and/or reinforced concepts I had already learned. As time passed, these teachings resonated with me and became so ingrained that it opened my heart wide to accept deep love once again, especially for myself. The synchronicity of Summer Bacon and the teachings of Dr. Peebles came at the most appropriate time for the next stage of my spiritual development. I am eternally grateful for Summer and for Dr. Peebles' work. It was through the encouragement of Dr. Peebles that I have begun to write.

****Both quotes from *This School Called Planet Earth*, by Summer Bacon, page XVII.**

Crystal Children – Refer to the Indigo Children definition below, as they are generally (but not always) the parents of the Crystal (Crystalline) children. The new youngsters being born, as described by Meg Blackburn Losey and others, live in the "NOW" since they have a different DNA, electromagnetic fields, consciousness levels and vibratory rates. They frequently demonstrate heightened levels of special gifts such as telepathy, empathy, intuition, and an acute sense of sensitivity with people and with everything in their environment.

Reverend Angela DeBry – This very influential spiritual teacher entered my life around 1985 and it has not been the same since. Angela became involved with a spiritual organization in the 1970's called "Solar Cross, A New Beginning," where she taught classes and channeled many of the extraterrestrial beings within the Galactic Federation plus many more. It was astonishing to me at that time that someone could do this and not be preachy about it. She always encouraged each student to search for his or her own path since all roads lead to the Source, and most importantly, to understand who you are and what you represent. The channeled teachings and information were from a higher dimensional realm and always contained a message of love. It resonated deeply within me as if tapping into old past-life memories that said; "Yes, I know this. I remember these universal truths." It all made sense and I knew it was right for me. I spent several years studying with Angela, learning about spirituality and healing from many metaphysical perspectives. Imagine having access to the incredible concepts of the 13 rays, 13 waves, galactic organizations of creation and the cast of galactic characters who govern them. We also explored other concepts such as multiple dimensions, karma, chakras, meditation, color healing, earth energies, and grid lines, as well as early civilizations and their sacred sites and time vaults such as Atlantis, Lemuria, and Sumeria. We also explored individual and collective missions for being born on earth at this time to allow for the clearing of old karmic energies and bringing in the new higher dimensions of energy for the rebirth of our planet. We studied the time lines for this clearing process of the physical, emotional, mental and spiritual bodies, which is still progressing today as outlined in this book. Many of us in the group traveled to many of the sacred sites to facilitate the clearing of the old karmic energies of the earth to begin to prepare for the new higher vibrations and the new children being born. We studied and traveled to the Yucatan Peninsula and worked on many of the Mayan ruins to shift the blocked energies and release trapped souls and reactivate the ancient time vaults. Next we traveled to England and Ireland where we visited the current site of Stonehenge, as well as its original site on the Aran Isles. Stonehenge was originally teleported off the Aran Isles and placed into its current location to create a loss of vibration and imbalance for the purposes of using fear and control. Again this dark energy needed to be shifted back to a place of balance. Our next trip was to Greece and the Island of Crete where the last known civilization, the Minoans, practiced a perfect balance between the male and female energies. The old ruins on Crete were some of the most interesting ruins I have seen on the planet. As you gaze upon their artwork, frescoes, and symbols, you can perceive the balance between the male and female attributes. Portrayed in the artwork that was produced shortly after that civilization's decline, you begin to see the degradation of the female body as it represented a loss of the feminine power. In addition, we also traveled to Athens and Delphi to clear the old energies in those locations. Later, our journeys took us to Sedona, Arizona, and Devil's Tower in Wyoming to clear the earth energies, as well as our own karma from past lives. Today, we don't physically travel to the sacred sites, but we all work energetically focusing, clearing, and invoking love around the planet and ourselves each day whenever we are telepathically called into duty. We each intuitively know our mission.

Overall, the classes, meditations, out-of-body experiences, and the interactions and love from many like-minded people are something I will cherish always. I am so much more than just a physical body. I now travel the world with my eyes and heart wide open knowing who I am and what I represent.

Dodecahedron – a 12-sided polyhedron with pentagonal faces. The sacred geometry of the number 12 has significance in that it represents 12 points of focus or reality and 12 aspects of God. By multiplying 12 x 12 x 12, this equates to 144,000 universes within each reality. I propose that perhaps an aspect of the divine God could possibly resemble a dodecahedron.

Etheric – Our etheric body is the exact counter-part to our physical body. This subtle essence or electromagnetic field represents our human energy field, also referred to as our **aura,** and resides outside of our physical body. This field of energy embodies our chakra system and other levels of awareness and consciousness. A **physical-etheric** being is one who dwells between both worlds of physical matter and a light, luminous, etheric one. At this time of transition on Earth, we will maintain our physical bodies, as we evolve into physical-etheric beings (moving from a carbon-based body to a silicon-based, crystalline form), using the full potential of our mind's capacity, not just a small portion of it as we are now.

Fifth Dimension – A dimension of light where we no longer embody physical matter, but a light, luminous, etheric body, resonating without duality, limitation or suffering.

Some refer to it as Heaven, yet I propose it portrays only the beginning of the dimensional ladder upward to the stars and beyond our imaginations.

Galactic Federation – According to Angela DeBry, our Milky Way galaxy is governed by the laws of the Universal Confederation of Planets, always following the laws of light, love, free will, and balance working in a positive and constructive manner. Members called a Tribunal, who oversee the implementation of these laws, govern our solar system and galaxy. One of these laws requires a non-interference decree in the internal affairs of a planet. However, after the destruction of Maldek, the law was adjusted to allow some interference; if destructive behavior on one planet was detected and could negatively affect other planets. The universal laws of free will, free choice and non-interference must be followed unless negative actions could possibly impact neighboring planets. When Earth's inhabitants fully awaken and transform to our higher minds of love, we will be invited to join the Galactic Federation.

Galactic history – By using this phrase, I am enticing you to expand your thinking beyond earth history and understand my reference to our Milky Way galaxy and beyond. What happens on Earth affects not only our galaxy but also the whole universe. What you do to change your life even in one small way influences the entire universe as well. You are that powerful.

Galactic wars – Eons ago, conflicts and wars occurred between the light and the dark in multiple universes, galaxies, solar systems, and planets.

God / Goddess / Big God – Notations of "God" with a capital "G" applies to the divine essence of the Supreme Being referred to by many names such as: Source, Radiant One, Everness, Oneness, Allah, Unlimitedness, Sacred Universal Breath, Infinity. The name can be whatever resonates with you. God, the divine essence, represents both the male and the female embodiments within perfect balance. Some prefer to relate to one aspect of the Supreme Being individually, referring to the feminine essence as the Goddess, or the masculine essence as God.

gods / goddesses / little gods – In using the example in the book "little gods" with a small "g," I am referring to the divinity of you and me by boldly suggesting we are gods in training to be masters such as the "Big God." The goal is to return to our original source of our soul embodiment, no longer in physical bodies of matter but uplifting back to our spiritual bodies and to a higher level of vibration and light as we continue to CO-CREATE.

God-self – the divine energy within every individual.

Golden Age – Also referred to as *graduation* or *ascension,* relating to the shift in consciousness on individual, planetary, galactic, universal and omniversal levels, manifested as a golden age of peace and harmony.

Great Awakening / Great Universal Awakening – All awakened beings shift consciousness and expand at once to a higher vibratory rate by moving from the Third Dimension to the Fourth, and then to the Fifth Dimension. Some also refer to this major shift in consciousness as "ascension." Others suggest we are shifting from the 3rd to the 12th dimension, which will require major changes at all levels of existence.

Higher Self – Your true soul/spiritual essence and many aspects of *self,* connected to your Over-Soul, managing several parts of you on all dimensions simultaneously creating a union with the divine God Source. See also definition of "soul-self."

Indigo Children – Lee Carroll and Jan Tober, authors of ***The Indigo Children, The New Kids have Arrived,*** speculate that the changes in children's behavior began to be noticed by adults, schools, and psychologists in the 1960's through the 1990's. These children were expressing "new and unusual psychological attributes showing patterns of behavior generally undocumented before." The old methods of rearing and disciplining these gifted children had to change as they responded to life in new ways. One theory proposes the new children (not all) incarnating around this time were being born more evolved spiritually, mentally, emotionally, and physically, and could not interact with our general society in the traditional manner since they were more empathic, telepathic, independent, and vividly aware that something was not right in our society. They are the "paradigm busters" as defined by Meg Blackburn Losey in her book ***The Children of Now.*** They are opening the doors to bring in the new, even more spiritually advanced children being born now, known as the Crystalline Children, Star Lights, and Star Children. (Refer to this Glossary for further definitions.)

Karma / duality – Karma is the law of action/inaction or cause and effect whereby a negative or positive act by one person must be re-experienced in a similar way by another to erase a previous imbalance. Duality represents the creation of positive/negative and light/ dark energies interacting many times manifesting karma.

Light Workers – Souls who volunteered to incarnate within this time frame on Planet Earth with the altruistic mission to transcend, transmute, and transform negativity by re-activating the universal laws of love, light, free will, and balance within our realm once again. These beings of light also chose to collectively incarnate into physical bodies on Earth at this time to facilitate the shift to the new Golden Age of the Grand Planetary and Universal Ascension for the good of all.

The roles are many as some choose to hold and ground the love and light, while others are demonstrations of free will and balance—all while mastering their own personal missions, karma, and lessons.

Millenials – Also referred to as Generation Y, this is a demographic group of children born between the 1980's and 2000. These children demonstrate an acute sense of community and tolerance and express a personal sense of fairness and empowerment.

Mote – This phrase "IT IS MY WILL SO MOTE THIS BE" and the specific word "mote" are old Wiccan expressions that connote a completion or sealing of the blessing.

Omni-universe – also called omniverse, representing multiple levels of universes, dimensions and parallels.

Orpheus Phylos – My first encounter with a metaphysical teacher who suddenly catapulted me onto the spiritual/metaphysical stage of my life was when I met Orpheus Phylos, who was teaching a seminar while channeling Archangel Michael. Over the years I have attended many of her seminars and lectures, enjoying such topics as the four elements of the earth, its grid patterns, ancient civilizations, the cosmos, extraterrestrials, planetary systems, and very important information about the coming new times of political and social upheavals, the individual and collective graduation, and ascension of Earth and the Universe. Not your everyday topics of conversation and definitely not on the nightly news. Imagine having the opportunity to talk with a spiritual guide about your past lives, the potential in this lifetime, and its purpose. It was amazing, and yet very difficult to comprehend at first. I was astonished to learn I was an oracle at Delphi (Greece) and a healer working with the fire element, a communicator, psychic, a star seed and more. Wow, these were astounding concepts for me to understand and to accept about myself. Over the years, I see these patterns of myself emerge as I allow for their possibility. Orpheus has been a wonderful teacher and friend for me and she has taught me so much over the years. Sadly, she transitioned in 2014—a dear friend and teacher who will be sorely missed.

Over-Soul – The head manager of all your higher selves at a spiritual level, interacting with all aspects of your lifetimes and multiple time lines occurring simultaneously.

Paranormal – Phenomena beyond a human's five senses and out of the range of scientific observation utilizing our sixth sense or intuition. Also referred to as a manifestation of a spiritual soul.

Dr. James Martin Peebles – is a spiritual guide and his messages of love are channeled through Summer Bacon. In his previous lifetime on earth (1823-1922), he was a writer, naturopath, medical doctor, spiritualist minister, and mystic. He chooses to continue his work on earth through trance channels such as Summer Bacon. (See Summer Bacon reference in Glossary for more detail.)

Psychic Reading – One who has the gift of perceiving/hearing/seeing from non-physical entities of the light who have transitioned (died) or exist on other dimensions, allowing the psychic to reveal insight and information from the spiritual realm. The process can be either at a conscious level or at a trance (unconscious) level, utilizing the vocal chords to communicate messages from spirit. This is not a possession but an agreement between the two souls to allow for such communication and, in most instances, a positive and enlightening experience.

Reincarnation – A religious or philosophical belief that after a physical body dies, its spirit/soul continues on and is reborn either in a physical body again or to other dimensions or realms. Many ancient and modern religions believe in reincarnation, and also refer to it as *transitioning* from one lifetime to the next.

Soul-self – Expression of the many aspects and root of Christ Consciousness—eternal flame and breath of oneness.

Star Children / Star Seeds – According to Orpheus Phylos, these are souls who chose to incarnate on Earth from other interplanetary star systems and realms expressing higher vibratory rates, levels of consciousness, and thought. Star Children are newer souls since they have not lived as many lifetimes on Earth as the Star Seeds. Both incarnated for the purpose of experiencing feeling and emotion on a personal level, but to also uplift and inspire humanity as they shift into the new Golden Age, clearing the old energies and thought patterns and progressing and enriching the way forward for the new schools of thought and existence on Planet Earth.

Star Lights – According to Orpheus Phylos, these are souls who have never experienced life in the cosmos. They began life through the evolutionary process on Planet Earth only. They now begin to invoke the process of awakening to the higher vibratory levels of consciousness as they prepare for the new Golden Age. Many choose to be schooled by the Star Seeds.

Third Dimension – A level of consciousness or a blueprint of creation perceived as dense physical matter vibrating at a solid energy frequency.

Third Eye – According to the Hindu Vedic philosophy, the physical body embodies seven primary chakras or energy centers. The Third Eye represents our psychic eye or sixth sense of our mental body located on the forehead between and slightly above the eyebrows.

Triad of Energy – Represents intent, data, and expression that brought forth the creation of physical and non-physical realities.

Universal Laws – The four laws are love, light, free will, and balance.

FOOTNOTES

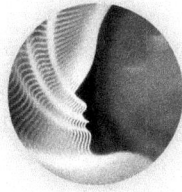

1. Dr. James Martin Peebles as channeled by trance medium, Summer Bacon. *This School Called Planet Earth*, Light Technology Publishing, Flagstaff, AZ, 2005. Page 322.
2. Ibid. Page 322.
3. Caroline Myss, "Energy Anatomy – The Science of Personal Power, Spirituality and Health." Concepts derived from Audio Tapes. Sounds True Publishing, Boulder, CO. 1997.
4. Shirley MacLaine, *Out on a Limb*, Bantam Books, New York, NY, 1983. She has several other books on the topic.
5. Angela DeBry, "Rainbow of Creations" lecture, 4/21/90. "Universal glue" term used to describe universal law of "love."
6. Dr. James Martin Peebles as channeled by trance medium, Summer Bacon. *This School Called Planet Earth*, Light Technology Publishing, Flagstaff, AZ, 2005.
7. Dannion Brinkley, "Saved by the Light," Villard Books, A division of Random House, New York, NY, 1994. He has several other books on this topic.
8. Dr. Grant H. Pealer, D.D., *Worlds Beyond Death*, Ozark Mountain Publishing, Huntsville, AR, 2007.
9. Alijandra, *Healing with the Rainbow Rays, The Art of Color Energy Therapy*, Emerald Star Publishing, San Jose, CA, 1995. Concepts paraphrased from pages 145-174. For further explanations and understandings of color, sound, movement and concepts explained in more detail, refer to this book.
10. Ibid. Page180. Also channeling information as channeled by Angela DeBry on 4/21/90 during "Rainbow of Creations" lecture.
11. Ibid. Pages 23-24 & 180-184. Also channeling information as channeled by Angela DeBry on 4/21/90 during "Rainbow of Creations" lecture.
12. These definitions were from Angela DeBry's "Rainbows of Creations" lecture and

channeling on 4/21/90. Concepts also explained by Alijandra, in her book *Healing with the Rainbow Rays, the Art of Color Energy Therapy*, as referenced above in Footnote 9 and 10.

13. Orpheus Phylos, "Teachings of Archangel Michael," Teachings and concepts paraphrased from a teleconference in November 2012. This meditation exercise is explained in the November 2012 monthly lecture.
14. Dr. James Martin Peebles as channeled by trance medium, Summer Bacon. *This School Called Planet Earth*, Light Technology Publishing, Flagstaff, AZ, 2005. Page 93. A favorite expression of Dr. Peebles is, "How do you like them apples?" This expression assists you to shift from deep, solemn contemplation to lightheartedness.
15. Ibid. Page XVII.
16. Ibid. Page 323.
17. Orpheus Phylos, "Teachings of Archangel Michael," Concepts and information derived from lecture on June 3, 2011.
18. Alijandra, *Healing with the Rainbow Rays, The Art of Color Energy Therapy*, Emerald Star Publishing, San Jose, CA, 1995. Page 176.
19. Angela DeBry, *UCM Quarterly*, Winter 2008 Vol. 27 No. 3, San Jose, CA. Page 22-23.
20. Alijandra, *Healing with the Rainbow Rays, The Art of Color Energy Therapy*, Emerald Star Publishing, San Jose, CA, 1995. Pages 18-32.
21. Angela DeBry, *UCM Quarterly*, Winter 2008 Vol. 27, No. 3, San Jose, CA. Pages 22-23. (Direct quote) Alijandra also referenced the information. Ibid.
22. Information channeled by DeBry and Alijandra (ibid) but paraphrased by author based on her interpretations and experiences.
23. Betty Bethards, *The Dream Book: Symbols for Self-Understanding*, The Inner Light Foundation, Novato, CA, 1983. Page 62.
24. Frances L. Ilg, M.D. and Louise Bates Ames, Ph.D., *The Gesell Institute's Child Behavior*, Harper & Row, New York, NY, 1955. Page 10.
25. Alijandra, *Healing with the Rainbow Rays, The Art of Color Energy Therapy*, Emerald Star Publishing, San Jose, CA, 1995. Pages 232 and 324. (The term "Over-Soul" used by Alijandra.) Ralph Waldo Emerson in his Essay "Over-Soul" coined this term.
26. Maia Kincaid, Ph.D. *Being Human & Loving Life, From the Wise Counsel of Plants, Animals, Insects & Earth,* Wisdom of Love Publishing, Sedona, AZ, 2009. Pages 1-6.
27. Robert Simmons & Naisha Ahsian, *The Book of Stones. Who they are and what they teach,* Heaven and Earth Publishing, East Montpelier, VT. 2005, Pgs. XVII-XVIII.
28. Sharon McErlane, *Our Love is our Power, Working with the Net of light that holds the Earth*, Net of Light Press. 2009.

29. Delores Cannon, *The Three Waves of Volunteers and the New Earth*, Ozark Mountain Publishing, Huntsville, AR. 2011, pg. 3,104 (E-Book).
30. Orpheus Phylos, "Teachings of Archangel Michael," Teachings and concepts paraphrased from a teleconference on January 21, 2011.
31. Louise L. Hay, *You Can Heal your Life*, Hay House Inc., Australia, 1984.
32. Ibid. Pages 151-152.
33. Dr. Grant H. Pealer, D.D., *World's Beyond Death*, Ozark Mountain Publishing, Huntsville, AR, 2007.
34. Orpheus Phylos and Virginia Essene, *Earth, the Cosmos and You. Revelations by Archangel Michael,* S.E.E Publishing Company, Santa Clara, CA, 1999. Pages 85-105. Information also channeled by Angela DeBry and Alijandra.
35. Orpheus Phylos and Virginia Essene, *Earth, the Cosmos and You. Revelations by Archangel Michael.* S.E.E Publishing Company, Santa Clara, CA, 1999. Pages 31-33.
36. Alijandra, *Healing with the Rainbow Rays, The Art of Color Energy Therapy*, Emerald Star Publishing, San Jose, CA, 1995. Pages 92-99. Also information provided by Angela DeBry, *UCM Quarterly,* Winter 2007, Vol. 26, No. 3, San Jose, CA. Pages 16-17, 42.
37. Lee Carroll and Jan Tober, *The Indigo Children, The New Kids Have Arrived,* Hay House, Carlsbad CA, 1999.
38. Meg Blackburn Losey, *The Children of Now, Crystalline Children, Indigo Children, Star Kids, Angels on Earth,* Career Press, Franklin Lakes, NJ. 2007.
39. These terms are referred to in the *Children of Now* and the *Earth, the Cosmos and You* books referenced above.
40. Information inspired by and derived from Little Grandmother Keisha Crowther. www.littlegrandmother.net.
41. Dr. James Martin Peebles as channeled by trance medium, Summer Bacon. *This School Called Planet Earth.* Light Technology Publishing, Flagstaff, AZ, 2005. Page 323.
42. J.J. Hurtak, *The Book of Knowledge: The Keys of Enoch,* The Academy for Future Science, Los Gatos, CA, 1977. Page 388.
43. Ken Keyes, Jr., *The Hundredth Monkey*, Vision Books, Coos Bay, Oregon, 1983. Page 5.
44. Ibid. Pages 10 -19.
45. Ibid. Page 17.

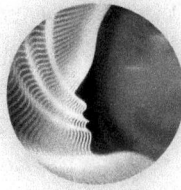

BIBLIOGRAPHY

1. Dr. James Martin Peebles as channeled by trance medium, Summer Bacon. *This School Called Planet Earth*, Light Technology Publishing, Flagstaff, AZ 2005. www.summerbacon.com.
2. Caroline Myss, "Energy Anatomy – The Science of Personal Power, Spirituality and Health." Concepts derived from Audio Tapes. Sounds True Publishing, Boulder, CO. 1997. www.myss.com.
3. Shirley MacLaine, *Out on a Limb*, Bantam Books, New York, NY, 1983. www.shirleymaclaine.com.
4. Dannion Brinkley, *Saved by the Light*, Villard Books, A division of Random House, New York, NY, 1994. www.dannion.com.
5. Dr. Grant H. Pealer, D.D., *Worlds Beyond Death*, Ozark Mountain Publishing, Huntsville, AR, 2007.
6. Alijandra, *Healing with the Rainbow Rays, The Art of Color Energy Therapy*, Emerald Star Publishing, San Jose, CA, 1995. www.colorhealing.com.
7. Channeling information as channeled by Angela DeBry on 4/21/90 during "Rainbow of Creations" lecture. www.sacredfoundations.net.
8. Orpheus Phylos, "Teachings of Archangel Michael," Concepts and information derived and paraphrased from lectures on January 21, 2011, June 3, 2011 and November 2012.
9. Angela DeBry, *UCM Quarterly*, Winter 2008, Vol. 27, No. 3. San Jose, CA. www.sacredfoundations.net.
10. Betty Bethards, *The Dream Book: Symbols for Self-Understanding*, The Inner Light Foundation, Novato, CA, 1983. www.bettybethards.com.
11. Frances L. Ilg, M.D. and Louise Bates Ames, Ph.D., *The Gesell Institute's Child Behavior*, Harper & Row, New York, NY, 1955.
12. Maia Kincaid, Ph.D. *Being Human & Loving Life, From the Wise Counsel of Plants, Animals, Insects & Earth*, Wisdom of Love Publishing, Sedona, AZ, 2009. www.maiakincaid.com.

13. Robert Simmons & Naisha Ahsian, *The Book of Stones, Who they are and what they teach,* Heaven and Earth Publishing, East Montpelier, VT, 2005.
14. Sharon McErlane, *Our Love is our Power, Working with the Net of light that holds the Earth*, Net of Light Press, 2009. www.grandmothersspeak.com
15. Delores Cannon, *The Three Waves of Volunteers and the New Earth*, Ozark Publishing, Huntsville, AR, 2011. www.delorescannon.com.
16. Louise L. Hay, *You Can Heal your Life*, Hay House Inc., Australia, 1984. www.louisehay.com.
17. Orpheus Phylos and Virginia Essene, *Earth, the Cosmos and You. Revelations by Archangel Michael,* S.E.E Publishing Company, Santa Clara, CA, 1999.
18. Angela DeBry, *UCM Quarterly*, Winter 2007, Vol. 26, No. 3, San Jose, CA. www.sacredfoundations.net
19. Lee Carroll and Jan Tober, *The Indigo Children, The New Kids Have Arrived,* Hay House, Carlsbad CA, 1999. www.indigochild.com.
20. Meg Blackburn Losey, *The Children of Now, Crystalline Children, Indigo Children, Star Kids, Angels on Earth,* Career Press, Franklin Lakes, NJ. 2007. www.spiritlite.com.
21. Information inspired by and derived from Little Grandmother Keisha Crowther. www.littlegrandmother.net
22. J.J. Hurtak, *The Book of Knowledge: The keys of Enoch*, The Academy for Future Science, Los Gatos, CA, 1977. www.keysofenoch.org.
23. Ken Keyes, Jr., *The Hundredth Monkey*, Vision Books, Coos Bay. Oregon, 1983.

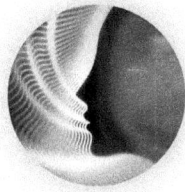

ABOUT THE AUTHOR
Dianne Hodges

Dianne Hodges has intuitively known for many years the importance of the Great Awakening and each of our roles in it, especially for our children and grandchildren. She believes that we cannot sit back any longer and watch the world go by. Instead, she says that we must now be active participants and create the world we want.

"We are the ones we have been waiting for" … as the American Indian elders tell us.

It is her own personal philosophies, explorations, and experiences, along with the spiritual awakening process, that motivated her to write this book to help others understand and trust their own inner knowing and empowerment. "We must *know* we are 'gods in training, co-creators of our world and beyond,'" she states.

Dianne is a Licensed and National Board-Certified Massage Therapist and Reiki Master with nearly 20 years experience who currently resides in Sedona, Arizona. A Universal Church of the Master Licentiate Minister (non-denominational) since 1995, she blended the healing touch of her hands with the emotional healing of spiritual counseling. In 2013, she transferred her ministerial credential to the Esoteric Interfaith Church, Inc., and joined as an ordained Inter-faith Minister to further her studies.

She has also worked in the corporate world in sales, marketing and management for print media and later in the health food industry. She earned her

Bachelor of Arts degree in journalism from the University of Minnesota in 1980.

Dianne has traveled to several sacred sites in many parts of the world and is fascinated by the wonderful similarities and differences between the ancient cultures. She is married with one grown daughter and two grandchildren.

www.ingramcontent.com/pod-product-compliance
Lightning Source LLC
LaVergne TN
LVHW051228080426
835513LV00016B/1464
* 9 7 8 0 6 9 2 4 5 2 3 6 3 *